JESUS'
WORD
JESUS'
WAY

*Grace & Love to you
in Christ,*

Randy K. Gasser

Randolph J. Klassen

JESUS' WORD JESUS' WAY

Foreword by Peter J. Dyck

HERALD PRESS
Scottdale, Pennsylvania
Waterloo, Ontario

Library of Congress Cataloging-in-Publication Data
Klassen, Randolph J.
   Jesus' Word, Jesus' Way / Randolph J. Klassen.
      p.   cm.
   Includes bibliographical references.
   ISBN 0-8361-3598-9
   1. Jesus Christ—Person and offices. 2. Mission of the church.
I. Title.
BT202.K49 1992
269'.2—dc20   92-13008
                                                   CIP

Scripture quotations are from the *Holy Bible: New International Version*. Copyright © 1973, 1978, 1984 International Bible Society. Used by permission of Zondervan Bible Publishers.

Quotations marked PHILLIPS are from *The New Testament in Modern English*, Revised Edition, © J. B. Phillips 1958, 1960, 1972. By permission of Macmillan Publishing Co., Inc., and William Collins Sons & Co., Ltd.

Quotations marked NEB are from *The New English Bible*. © The Delegates of the Oxford University Press and the Syndics of the Cambridge University Press 1961, 1970. Reprinted with permission.

JESUS' WORD, JESUS' WAY
Copyright © 1992 by Herald Press, Scottdale, Pa. 15683
   Published simultaneously in Canada by Herald Press,
   Waterloo, Ont. N2L 6H7. All rights reserved
Library of Congress Catalog Number: 92-13008
International Standard Book Number: 0-8361-3598-9
Printed in the United States of America
Book and cover design by Paula M. Johnson

1 2 3 4 5 6 7 8 9 10 98 97 96 95 94 93 92

to
my wife, Joyce,
six kids—Timothy, Stephen, Jonathan, Jeff,
Wendi, Gregg—and the congregation of
Good Samaritan Community Covenant Church

Contents

Foreword

North Americans are a success-oriented people. We want to win in sports, war, business, and the pulpit. Anything wrong with that? Jesus was success-oriented. He knew that to succeed you need power, so he told his disciples, "You will receive power" (Acts 1:8). There is no automatic virtue in weakness.

Two questions arise: What methods do we employ in the struggle to win? And what is the end product? In this book, Randolph Klassen examines the implications of these questions for the church, its members, and its leaders. Is there growth in our churches, he asks? And are the methods for growth biblical?

Jesus had fed 5,000 people. The next day they followed him to Capernaum and asked, "Rabbi, when did you get here?" But Jesus knew they could care less when he got there. What they meant was, "Rabbi, when do we get another free lunch?" Jesus' answer clearly reflects their expectations. "You are looking for me, not because you saw miraculous signs but because you ate the loaves and had your fill" (John 6:26).

We still want a free lunch. In South Korea a church has quickly grown to half a million members because it preaches salvation, health, and prosperity. In the

United States, the government had to stop the glitz-and-showbiz TV evangelist who was building a financial empire for himself with his "gospel" preaching.

Growth to many North Americans means a rise in numbers—whether of dollars, cars, or church members. To say this should not be our goal is tantamount to being unpatriotic. Such methods are unbiblical and their products questionable.

Klassen confronts such problems as Charles Sheldon did long ago in his book, *In His Steps.* Sheldon urged Christians to ask, "What would Jesus do?" Too simple? Klassen doesn't think so. His concern throughout his book is that the *message* (spoken and acted) and *method* be those of the Master, Jesus Christ. Hence the appropriate title, *Jesus' Word, Jesus' Way.*

Klassen invites us to look carefully at ourselves, our church, and our ministry. Is Jesus' word truly proclaimed in Jesus' way? We need to be alert, lest we unwittingly take over the world's goals and methods.

This excellent book is easy to read and liberally sprinkled with anecdotal material. It lends itself to private and group study in home and church. The reader will never be able to avoid the two central questions: What is the mission of the church? What are the right methods for carrying out the mission?

And what goes for the church goes also for each individual Christian. Is what I am saying in word and deed really Jesus' word? And am I saying and doing it in Jesus' way?

—*Peter J. Dyck*
Akron, Pennsylvania

Author's Preface

This is not a book about "getting results," "methods that work," or "successful techniques" in building the church. Hundreds of such books have been written in recent decades. Their contributions have been valuable. Through them, churches have been challenged to plan, mobilize, and implement effective growth strategies. As time passes, the culture and problems facing the church change—requiring changes in approach, technique, and methodology. That is the thesis of such books—and it is undoubtedly partly true.

This book, however, is about the other part, the part we too often assume we know. I refer to those unchanging principles we find in the style, manner, and methods of Jesus as he shares God's good news. I want to study these features of Jesus with you, so that we can let his ways judge, correct, and guide our ways.

My fear is that, especially in the Western world, we have made too many glib assumptions about our faith. We assume Jesus would approve our affluent lifestyles, elaborate liturgies, beautiful church buildings, scholarly seminaries, Sunday services, church growth conferences, TV ministries, evangelistic campaigns. After all, we do all this "in his name and for his glory."

Are these assumptions justified? Church history provides ample evidence of how people called Christians have interpreted the gospel through culture-colored glasses stained with their prejudices. This has resulted in a fruit bearing little or no resemblance to the vine. Time and again, instead of bowing to Jesus' way, we bend his approach to fit our preferred pattern.

So "Christians" have tortured dissenters, burned "witches," killed "infidels," and forced at sword point the baptism of entire villages—all "in his name," of course. Today, still "in his name," we manipulate crowds to get them to "come forward." We justify segregation as God's order. We smile at the pastor in his Rolls Royce ("he deserves it") and we defend altars of gold in towns of starving people.

I could not help but chuckle when I heard a middle-class preacher tell his middle-to-upper-class congregation, that Jesus was not a laborer. "In the Greek," he explained, "the word 'carpenter' meant 'contractor.' "

That put Jesus in the correct class category. The Jesus who owned no pillow was not in that sermon! We must be constantly aware of this tendency. Instead of letting Jesus shape our manners and methods, we call on him to baptize with his approval the techniques we have already chosen. We still want to do it our way.

Jesus said, "I am the way, and the truth, and the life" (John 14:6). One translator phrases it, "I am the true and living way." Manner, method, and message merge in Jesus. His truth is not authentically communicated unless it is garbed and shared in a way fully consistent with his style and character. To say that the gospel is changeless—whereas the methods of presenting it must change with each generation—is dangerous oversimplification.

Certainly the core principles of the gospel are time-less. What I wish to affirm is that principles of sharing the faith are equally timeless, because they belong to the essence of the gospel. So the following study is a careful look at how Jesus shared God's good news. Comparisons with our ways will be made, for better or for worse. The hope is that we will let Jesus judge our practices and establish our priorities.

The results may be dangerous. It could mean a smaller rather than a larger church membership! It could mean a radical change in the order of Sunday services, the schedule of church meetings, the place of the home, the concept of stewardship, and the methods of evangelism. Whatever the changes, the results must look more like Jesus Christ, if any new forms are to be accepted as valid.

Finally, I want to admit a personal reason for writing this book. About a decade ago, I left pastoral ministry because of serious personal failure. I became a profes-sional artist.

Then some years ago, I led a home Bible study using the Gospel of Luke. Our aim was to become better ac-quainted with Jesus. The interest and size of the group grew. Today, we are an exciting fellowship of believers called Good Samaritan Community Covenant Church. The name, which also describes our mission, came out of our Bible study in Luke.

Now, in a move I believe was directed by God, I am back in the pastoral role. I am grateful for the measure of healthy growth the church has experienced. But I also feel an uneasiness about how things are going. Are we really doing it Jesus' way? Is the growing membership a sign of God's blessing? Are we following Jesus' design for the building of his church?

This book is not about our church as a model. It is about our mutual struggle to separate the chaff from the wheat as we explore what constitutes an authentic church. I want the reader to investigate with me those lines of New Testament evidence that will lead to a church which follows the divine design.

We shall ask our Lord about his manner and approach. We will consider several areas that relate to the church's sharing of the gospel. We will look at

- his way of identifying with others,
- his balance of word and deed,
- his use of Scripture and advertising,
- his invitation to discipleship,
- his sense of urgency and understanding of ultimate destiny.

Finally we shall study his teaching tools and how he offered himself to God in prayer and worship, the supreme priority of his life.

I invite you to explore with me. We want to become better acquainted with Jesus. If this happens, we will love him more and serve him more faithfully by exploring Jesus' word, Jesus' way.

—*Randolph J. Klassen*
Valley Springs, California

JESUS' WORD
JESUS' WAY

Chapter One

Jesus Identified with Sinners

Few features are more clear from the gospels than that Jesus related to sinful people. He was and is one with us, with the focus of his identity being on the "lowest and the least." Although sinless himself, he seems more at home with "sinners" than "the righteous."

This identity was hinted at from the beginning, as his genealogy in Matthew indicates. The table of names not only includes women (unexpected for a "pure" lineage) but four "irregular" women. They are Tamar, Rahab, Ruth, and Bathsheba—a Canaanite, a Jericho prostitute, a Moabite, and a Hittite. These were hardly people included to underscore racial purity! As Rob Peterson points out, "not only is Jesus born for sinners, but he is born through sinners."[1] This is underscored by the women and men Matthew includes in Jesus' genealogy.

Jesus is "flesh of our flesh." He wet his diapers (or their first-century equivalents) and cried for his next feeding as any child does. As we all must, he had to study to learn, work to achieve, and pray to be strong. He struggled and suffered with every temptation common to humanity. He is one of us.

Now if anyone had any right to avoid this identity he did—but chose not to. Yet we, who have no right to avoid it, seem to make every effort to sidestep the confession of weakness. Tragically, it is often when we camouflage our weaknesses and failures that we hinder communication of God's grace.

Who can relate to one who gives the impression of "having arrived"? Does the pulpit really suggest, as one member put it, that the pastor "stands six feet above contradiction"? We cannot all identify with the successful, but we can relate to one who admits weakness. Jesus accepted our weakness.

Jesus prepares for ministry

There are fanciful stories of Jesus as a know-it-all youth, but they are in ancient records that were never part of the biblical witness. Little is known of his boyhood. Luke tells us that when he was in the temple at age twelve, he was "listening" to the teachers and "asking them questions" (Luke 2:46). They were amazed at his understanding, but they were not offended by any trace of youthful arrogance. Except for this growing wisdom and commitment to his Father's will, he was like other young people around him. He knew and knows the feelings, trials, and temptations of youth.

It was as a youth in the temple that Jesus recognized he was called to accomplish a special mission for his heavenly Father (Luke 2:49). He probably knew the story behind his name (Matt. 1:21). Mary had, no doubt, shared with him the wonderful things that had happened in the days surrounding his birth.

Yet it was not until he was thirty that Jesus left the carpenter shop to commence his public ministry. The question must be raised, "If he knew he was to be the world's Savior, why did he wait so long?"

We can speculate about Jesus' willingness to assume family responsibilities. Tradition tells us that Joseph had died, probably during Jesus' teen years. Jesus, being the oldest child, would probably have shouldered the chief responsibilities in the home. No doubt there were bills to pay and several younger brothers and sisters to feed and clothe. That could be one reason his public ministry seemed delayed.

Still, if we transfer our contemporary impatience to his day, we probably would call him to action much sooner. Can you not imagine some zealous young "Christian" telling Jesus to stop wasting his time in the carpenter shop while "the world is going to hell"? This zealot might quote Paul: "Now is the time of God's favor, now is the day of salvation!"

But Jesus calmly continued to turn out tables and benches for his neighbors. Apparently our sense of urgency is not the same as his. Or have we missed the value of the right kind of preparation? What does this say about his identification with us?

Jesus was not called to public ministry until eighteen years after his temple revelation. If we trust a wisdom in God's timing, then we may see an extremely important ingredient in this preparation period for Jesus. He was the village carpenter. He was experiencing what the other townsfolk experienced—family squabbles, family reunions, weddings, funerals, business failures, economic successes, lean times, busy times, politics, and religion. He was involved in all of it. The people knew him. He knew them. There was a common bond. They were all Nazarenes and Galileans. He matured at their side as one with them. It was key to his preparation, this full identification with his own people.

Jesus' years of maturation make me wonder if prior to or after seminary training, candidates for the ministry ought to spend several years in the world at some secular job. Then they could more fully appreciate the tensions and pressures of those who will be in their congregations. We may read *The Secular City*, and even grasp its contents, but we are not really in the secular world until we live there.

Maybe there should be no ordinations until age thirty. Which older minister has not been embarrassed by reading early sermons and recalling early blunders? Maturity does not come automatically with the years, but maybe a little more experience of the mix and madness of this world would help.

Jesus identifies with sinners

Once Jesus had experienced the world, he was finally ready to leave the carpenter shop for a larger arena. He stepped out with a dramatic act—he was baptized by John.

John was calling all people to repent and prepare for the kingdom of God that was "near" (Matt. 3:2). Baptism was a sign of their cleansing and was offered not only to proselytes (as previously been the case) but especially, at this time, to Jews. To receive baptism, a per-

son both confessed sinfulness and demonstrated repentance.

Then John saw Jesus coming toward him in the water to be baptized. John was startled. "I need to be baptized by you, and do you come to me?" (Matt. 3:14).
But Jesus insisted that only if John baptized him could
God's purposes be fulfilled.

So in Jesus' first public action he was specifically
identified with sinners. The prophet had foretold that
the Messiah would be "numbered with the transgres-
sors" (Isa. 53:12). That identity had now begun. God
was pleased and symbolized his anointing with the
dove-like descent of the Holy Spirit upon Jesus. Then
a voice from heaven said, "This is my Son, whom I
love; with him I am well pleased" (Matt. 3:17).

Maybe God would be more pleased with his servants today if we were more willing to affirm a solidarity with all people. Theological training is good, but
there is no substitute for a real identity with people.
That was Jesus' way. It was also the style of the apostle
Paul. He could confess that his struggle was real (Rom.
7); that he couldn't get the thorn out of his "flesh,"
(2 Cor. 12:7) and that he felt like the worst of sinners.
(1 Tim. 1:15). But Paul also earned the "well done" of
his Lord.

This identification with humanity is the incarnational theme that began at Jesus' birth and continued
to the grave. The carpenter shop is a vital part of this
theme. Then baptism put the theme in neon lights.
And the cross gave it an exclamation point!

Jesus' ministry consistently exemplified his
identification with humanity. The common people en-

joyed listening to him. He ate and drank with tax collectors and sinners. He was charged with being a friend of the unwashed and unsavory types. "This man welcomes sinners and eats with them" (Luke 15:2). The charge was true.

Do we identify with sinners as Jesus did?

How does our identity with people compare with Jesus? David Watson once wrote, quoting Leighton Ford,

> Many Christians have been so afraid of being contaminated by worldliness that they have avoided any social contacts with unconverted persons. As a result, they have no natural bridges for evangelism. What witnessing they do is usually artificial and forced rather than the spontaneous outgrowth of genuine friendship. . . . Part of Jesus' attractiveness . . . was his wonderful love of life, his natural appealing friendliness. Luke shows Jesus going from dinner party to dinner party, teaching the gospel to the guests. If Jesus came back today and mingled with gamblers, the skid-row crowd, and the cocktail set, a lot of shocked Christians would throw up their hands and say he was too worldly!"[2]

We are not "of" the world but are to be "in" the world, the world God loves. As Becky Pippert notes in *Out of the Salt Shaker*, Christians fail their role as the salt of the earth if they remain in the container. Sometimes we need to be shaken to identify with our neighbors as Jesus identified with his.

One church growth principle has to do with linking a congregation to its community. The bridge between believers and nonbelievers cannot be built unless there is an understanding of and affirmation of the people for whom the good news is intended.

Do the people in our community know that we Christians have trials and temptations, hopes and fears similar to theirs? Or do they think of us as a strange group of religious types who stick to themselves and think they are better than others?

Jesus so loved the common people that he didn't care what reputation he developed with the religious elite. His identity with sinners became an affirmation of them as persons of infinite value.

Jesus made people feel hopeful. Whether poor blind Bartimaeus, wealthy lonely Zachaeus, or "that crazy lady of Magdala," Mary—Jesus affirmed them all. To become his disciples, Jesus called Matthew the compromiser, and Simon the fiery Zealot. He called Thomas, the skeptical Galilean, and Judas, the accountant from Judea. He made each feel special.

Jesus continued to affirm sinners until his death. From the cross he offered pardon to all (Luke 23:34) although we read of no one asking for it. Then he turns to the criminal hanging on the cross beside him, who does ask to be remembered. Jesus promises him all that "today you will be with me in paradise" could possibly mean (Luke 23:43).

The repentant thief on the cross felt he could turn to Jesus because Jesus would understand his situation. Do people feel free to come to the church, to their Christian neighbors, or a local pastor with confidence that they will be accepted and understood? Identity helps create empathy. The one who has traveled a road is the one to whom we will turn when we must travel the same road.

There can be no authentic communication of the gospel apart from a full immersion in the human stream. Our Lord identified with sinners. We are his body. We therefore can do no less. Just dropping tracts from the sky won't do. If such a travesty occurred, we would probably find Jesus among the concerned citizens sweeping up the unwanted clutter.

The incarnation affirms the marvelous paradox of Jesus' identification with both sinful humans and holy God! In Jesus, God is revealed. In Jesus, God is revealed *to us*. In Jesus, we see God's grace and truth in terms we can begin to grasp. In Jesus, word described deed—and deed clarified word—making communication powerful. In Jesus we see God's hand of welcome outstretched to us. Jesus was God's evangelistic "method."

Making God visible

This then is the test for our witness. Does it make the living God visible in terms our neighbors can understand?

God has used Chuck Colson to reach the inmates of many prisons in America. Because Colson was once a prisoner himself, he can identify with other prisoners. Colson's experience of their situation enables them to hear more clearly and trust more readily the news he shares.

We should not all become prisoners to reach prisoners, or alcoholics to reach alcoholics, of course. But there is a solidarity with all people that exists and needs to be affirmed. We are fellow creations in the divine image, co-sinners, equally vulnerable, equally in need of pardon. We are equally bound for death and a meeting with our Maker. Above all, we are equally loved by God. We have more than enough in common to establish identity with anyone.

The church has often failed to stress this commonality with all persons. We have adopted a pharisaic position toward others under the guise of sanctification, interpreting it to mean separation from sinners—instead of from sinful ways. We fail to let Jesus be our guide to what holiness really means. Somehow his involvement with people and their culture goes right past us.

We think we are close to God when we mount our pedestals of high sounding taboos and disassociate from sinners. These negations result in a negation of the very ones we are called to affirm in the love of Christ. Separated from sinners, we believe we are closer to our Lord when, in fact, we are further from him, for he is always a "friend of sinners." He is where the needy are. We also must be there to invite sinners into God's presence.

Like Jesus, believers are also called to stand against those who oppress and with those who are the oppressed. God's people, if they truly belong to him, belong to his causes of justice and righteousness in the earth. If God attacked the sin problem with the arsenal of total identification with us in suffering love, can we think of a better way? A safer one—yes—but not a better one!

What does this suggest that the church must do regarding a group of exploited laborers, a disenfranchised race, a community suffering from disease and hunger? Some third-world churches speak of Christ as "Liberator," meaning he has come not only for all sinners but particularly for those "sinned against." Jesus is present in a church that shares the struggles of the poor and oppressed.

Admittedly the church must avoid taking sides with one group of people against another, for all are loved by God. But the church, when faithful to Jesus, will identify more closely with those whose needs are most pressing and burdensome. Jesus blessed the poor. His body is called to the same ministry. The kingdom is really here, Jesus assured John, because among other things, "the good news is preached to the poor" (Matt. 11:5). They heard him because he was one with them.

Something like that happened decades ago in a tenement district along the south side of Roosevelt Avenue in Chicago. My cousin Herb and a couple of his Christian companions felt God's leading to share the good news in this area. They rented an apartment, patched the rat holes, and dressed in the common gray denims worn by most of the men in that area. They frequented the local pool hall, and invited their new friends over for soup and bread.

Their presence was met with understandable suspicion. "What are these 'honky dudes' doing here?" the residents wondered. It took a long time to establish trust. Earning it would prove costly.

My friends were threatened, mugged, and robbed. Such an experience only gave them greater empathy for other victims of crime, of which there were many in that community.

The turning point came when Herb contacted an absentee landlord about his dangerously dilapidated vacant property. Could they clean it up and turn it into a children's playground? Permission was granted. Work began with some pool hall friends and soup supper companions assisting.

Some still wondered, "Why are they doing this?" Most of us have difficulty understanding unconditional love. It is so rare. But it was there. Families became believers as they watched their children play in a healthy and safe atmosphere. The word got out, "Don't hurt those boys. They're okay. They're on our side."

That is identification Jesus-style! That is how the first church went about its witness. It lived by the formula, "as any had need" (Acts 2:45). This sharing met with "favor of all the people. And the Lord added to their number daily those who were being saved" (Acts 2:47).

This identity with people in their needs was one key to fruitfulness of the early church. It is always good news to have one's needs met. A community sensitive to human need is a "good news community." It is ready to pay the cost of loving service. It has chosen the way of him who "though he was rich, yet for your sakes he became poor, so that you through his poverty might become rich" (2 Cor. 8:9).

Jesus identified with sinners. That bridged the gap and brought them hope. The question I ask myself is, "Does my witness proceed from such an affirmation of oneness with those I meet?" "Does our church affirm an identity with this community where God has placed us and in which we are called to bear witness?"

Only so shall Jesus' word proceed in his way.

Reflection

Is Jesus' identification with the people obvious in the attitudes of our congregation toward *all* people?

It is fascinating to notice that persons of all "minority" groups mentioned in the New Testament receive affirmation from Jesus. There is not a single negative comment from him about Romans, Greeks, Samaritans, tax collectors, women, or children. Instead, Jesus praises members of each of these groups!

How does our social outlook compare to that of our Lord?

Chapter Two

Jesus Balanced Word and Deed

When we define evangelism as having to do primarily with proclaiming "the good news," we are no doubt correct. John R. W. Stott says, "Evangelism may and must be defined only in terms of the message."[3] Jesus used the word *evangelisesthai* when he defined his mission as preaching "good news to the poor" (Luke 4:18).

Communication is more than words

This is the emphasis in communicating the message of the gospel. However, the art of communication calls for grounding the gospel in real life. Truly communicating the message requires *demonstration* in addition to description of the gospel.

More than words are involved in communication. One educator has claimed that words alone account for less than a tenth of what makes for effective communication. The enacted sermon is the one most easily understood. The visual demonstration is the most powerful validation of the verbal discourse.

Furthermore, the message we bring is not a string of ideas, but a witness to a person—with the announcement that this Person transforms persons. Thus maybe we have not announced the message at all until we have given some personal demonstration of Christ's transforming power!

The good news is Jesus Christ himself. Since this is the case, can we really speak of having communicated the gospel if we have offered only rational discourse? Folks may understand an *idea* this way, but they cannot meet a *person* this way. If we are called to introduce people to Jesus Christ, the least we must do is let them *see* something of Jesus through our words.

God himself has always been impatient with words alone. Throughout the Old Testament God resorted to visual demonstrations and enacted proclamations. He commissioned Moses through a burning bush. He warned the Egyptians through a series of plagues. He assured Israel of his guiding presence through a cloud by day and a pillar of fire at night. The commandments at Sinai were given with thunder and lightning.

God is the God of history; the God who acts. He is not a philosopher god who sits in solitude pondering his own perfection, as would Aristotle's "Prime Mover, himself unmoved." He is the God who speaks in action. At the pivotal events of redemption, as in the original event of creation, word and deed become one!

"In the past God spoke to our forefathers through the prophets at many times and in various ways, but in these last days he has spoken to us by his Son" (Heb. 1:1-2). That is as personal and as direct as God could get.

"The Word became flesh and made his dwelling among us," John exclaims (John 1:14). Then John goes on to say that the "grace and truth" of God has been communicated. It has been seen in three-dimensional richness! "No one has ever seen God, but God the One and Only, who is at the Father's side, has made him known" (John 1:18). We read Jesus and the message is the heart of God. To know the Son is to know the Father (John 14:9).

Evangelism is words—and more

God communicates his good news not primarily through reasoned argument, but by the incarnation of his Son. When God addresses us in our language of flesh and blood we begin to understand what he means by "grace and truth." Communication happens when the Word becomes flesh. In this sense one must insist that evangelism demands more than words.

It is irresponsible to suggest that evangelism is "everything the church does in the world." It is equally inadequate to sigh that there are as "many definitions for evangelism as there are evangelists." These definitions cannot equally rate biblical validity.

Terms like *mission* or *witness* do encompass the church's areas of loving service in the world. But evangelism is not synonymous with social action. You can reform, but you cannot "evangelize" a social structure or political system—you can only evangelize persons.

Yet in a healthy church, can one concern really exist

without the other? Can evangelism be truly a proclamation of good news if at the same time social, physical, and material needs of persons are ignored? It
seems to me that the deed of love is so inextricably
linked to the spoken message that the deed is what
determines the validity of the word.

The mandate of love decrees that we do what adds
to the well-being of another. Love reaches out to give
that which makes another whole. It looks for opportunity to serve. Being touched by such love is being
touched by God's grace. The outreach of love will
involve both word and deed. We may call the verbal-
ized expression of the gospel *evangelism*. But whether
the words truly communicate what God intends may
depend entirely on an incarnation of God's grace, on
some visible and tangible expression of the reality of
Christ.

Some evangelical writers seem so fearful of overem-
phasis on social involvement that they insist on putting social concern under evangelism as a secondary
or even lower element of the church's ministry in the
world. They sometimes suggest that social action may
be a good preparation for evangelism—as "a door
opener," or as a consequence of evangelism. But these
works are not seen as equal to evangelism in the mission of the church. Some still insist that "historically
the mission of the church is evangelism alone."[4] This
thesis is contradicted by the teaching and example of
Jesus.

When the love of Christ is our motive and the example of Christ our model, we cannot put any genuine act
of love in a second-class category. The first and great

commandment calls for love of God and neighbor.

At a National Association of Evangelicals conference, I heard that "the great commission" takes precedence over "the great commandment." Such an assertion follows a strange principle of biblical interpretation. The Bible does not teach neighbor love that exalts soul concerns and denies the needs of the body. Jesus does not say that at the final judgment the question will be how many converts we have made. What will count are acts of love the faithful offered to the least of Jesus' brothers and sisters—and thus to him (Matt. 25:31-46).

Paul's classic exaltation of love in 1 Corinthians 13 celebrates the ethic of the kingdom of our Jesus. The New Testament repeatedly defines our life and mission as loving others like we have been loved. "If anyone has material possessions and sees his brother in need but has no pity on him, how can the love of God be in him?" (1 John 3:17). The answer of the early church was unanimous: "Whoever does not love does not know God, because God is love" (1 John 4:8).

Jesus balanced word and deed

E. J. Carnell observed, "Jesus defined an ethic that is final for all time, for there is no conceivable way in which an advance can be made on the law of love."[5] This "royal law" always calls forth words *and* actions. It is not surprising to see in Jesus' own proclamation of the good news that a fine balance of word and deed distinguishes his ministry.

A quick reading through Matthew's Gospel, with its heavy emphasis on the teachings of Jesus, reveals thirty-four instances of gracious deeds accompanied by few words. Although recorded in fuller detail, the number of teaching situations is approximately thirty-three.

In Mark we are again struck by a similar balance of act and word. Mark records twenty-eight gracious acts, including eighteen miracles (mostly exorcisms), and about twenty-nine teaching occasions (more briefly described than in Matthew).

Luke and John admittedly don't quite fit the pattern. Luke identifies at least thirty-five gracious actions and about forty-two teaching situations. However, he describes his Gospel as one that tells of "all that Jesus began *to do* and to teach" (Acts 1:1, italics added).

John, who recalls so much of Jesus' personal sharing with his disciples, describes about seventeen teaching situations. He records fourteen acts of grace and mercy.

The actual statistics will vary with those who peruse the text, but the comparison will always be close enough to make the same point. The good news of the kingdom came supported and validated by the actions which signaled the defeat of evil and death itself. In this sense, Jesus was a holistic evangelist.

Look at only two chapters of Matthew and recall how with few or no words Jesus was good news to

- The centurion—Jesus healed his servant (Matt. 8:5-13).
- Simon's mother-in-law—Jesus healed her (Matt. 8:14-17).
- The disciples in the storm—Jesus calmed the sea (Matt. 8:23-27).

- The Gadarene demoniac—Jesus exorcised the legion (Matt. 8:28-34).
- The paralytic—Jesus healed him (Matt. 9:1-8).
- The publicans at Levis' party—Jesus went with joy (Matt. 9:10-13).
- The woman with the hemorrhage—Jesus healed her (Matt. 9:20-22).
- The daughter of Jairus—Jesus raised her from death (Matt. 9:18-26).
- Two blind men—Jesus opened their eyes (Matt. 9:27-31).
- The dumb man—Jesus set him free to speak (Matt. 9:32-34).
- Many people—Jesus healed them (Matt. 9:35).

So many acts—yet Matthew specializes in Jesus' teachings!

The comments of the people reinforced the fact that action and preaching were inseparable elements of Jesus' ministry. The reaction of the people to Jesus is recorded like this: "Where did this man get these things? . . . What's this wisdom that has been given him, that he even does miracles!" (Mark 6:2). Wisdom and mighty works were recognized as belonging to each other.

Luke records a similar response in phrasing that makes word and deed synonymous. "All the people were amazed and said to each other, 'What is this teaching? With authority and power he gives orders to evil spirits and they come out'" (Luke 4:36).

David Watson comments perceptively that "although the verb to 'evangelize,' when strictly translated, means no more than to announce good news, it is unthinkable in the ministry of Jesus to separate the active verb from the action in which it is set.'"[6]

Talking about love is easier than enacting it. Correcting someone's theology is less costly than helping a person find health, work, or justice. The church is not the body of Christ if it specializes in proclamation void of demonstration. Conversely it cannot focus on activism void of proclamation. The church was known as those who "devoted themselves to the apostles' teaching and to the fellowship, to the breaking of bread and to prayer" (Acts 2:42).

The church must join word and deed

The church was equally known for "the signs and wonders" done through the apostles, as well as for the actions of love which led to a total sharing of material resources so that all were ministered to "as any had need" (Acts 2:45). This balanced witness of word and deed reveals a healthy church, through which the Lord could add "to their number daily those who were being saved" (Acts 2:47).

The church is called to be good news to those it meets. Jesus said to his followers, "As the Father has sent me, I am sending you" (John 20:21). The way Jesus fulfilled his mission is the model for us. That style is incarnational—the word becomes flesh, speech becomes deed, thought becomes action. The gospel is both proclaimed and demonstrated.

This joining of word and deed was experienced by a young African I met at the University of California (at Davis). He had become a Christian through the witness of a Mennonite mission in Ethiopia. To my question about how this happened, he replied that the people of the mission didn't just preach. "They loved us."

When I pressed for more details, he told about the medical, agricultural, and educational help these Christians had provided. When he learned that Jesus Christ was who motivated them to do this, he felt eager to know this one who could make such a beautiful difference in the way people behaved.

How have our churches balanced word and deed? What changes need to be made in our churches to enable our communities to see as well as hear the good news? Are we sharing Jesus' word, Jesus' way?

Reflection

What do you think of this approach by a developer pastor? He went door to door in his community, not asking anyone to come to his church, give anything, or join anything. He simply asked if the people had any needs or desires with which the church might help. He cited a few illustrations of what he meant, so that they would not think he had only their spiritual needs in mind. He compiled a long list! Equally important was that the people of his community found out that the church cared—cared even about jobs, child care, alcoholism, transportation to an outpatient clinic, and the quality of public school education!

Jesus balanced word and deed as Servant-Savior. How can our church assume his servant style in our neighborhood?

Chapter Three

Jesus Used His Bible

That Jesus used Scripture is well known. How he used it is not so well known. Yet knowledge of Jesus' Scripture use is crucial for any healthy understanding of the Bible by the church.

The Bible plays an indispensable role in the life and witness of the church. Apart from it there is no evangel to proclaim. If we preach a Christ unlike the Jesus of the gospels, we describe an alien messiah. Only the biblical Jesus Christ is authentic. How we use the Scripture therefore determines how we will perceive, interpret, and apply the gospel.

I'll never forget how one man, whom I met on Portage Avenue in Winnipeg, interpreted Scripture. He was a self-styled prophet carrying a sandwich-board sign on which was printed, in crude lettering, "Escape the Abomination of Desolation."

Curiosity pushed me to ask him how I might escape.

His reply was direct. "Follow the teachings of Jesus," he said.

I thanked him and assured him that such was my intention.

He gave me a doubtful look, then said, "You cannot get married if you follow Jesus."

I couldn't recall anything like that, so I asked him where he found it.

"Don't you know the Lord's Prayer?" he retorted.

I did, but the teaching of celibacy had eluded me.

He enlightened me. "It says, 'Thy will be done on earth as it is in heaven,' and Jesus also said, 'They neither marry nor are given in marriage in heaven.' So if you are going to obey Jesus, you will not get married!"

His argument was amazing. Since then I have seen how, time and again, a literalistic interpretation can produce peculiar doctrines.

This is one reason the average Christian and the biblical scholar must remain in close and friendly association. We need each other. If evangelistic zeal seems sometimes lacking in the professor of biblical theology, so is biblical integrity sometimes lacking in the would-be herald of the gospel. James Denny says, "If evangelists were our theologians and theologians were our evangelists we would come nearer to the ideal church." We must make constant reference to our primary sources, our biblical roots, if we are to be faithful interpreters of the gospel.

Our message is Jesus Christ—the Christ of Matthew, Mark, Luke, John, Peter, James, and Paul. We rely on their record to tell us about Jesus. Studying their accounts and learning to know Jesus through them, we arrive at certain convictions regarding Jesus' person, teachings, and actions. Among his teachings are references to Scripture which enable us to come to a view of the written word in harmony with his testimony regarding it. For the Christian, Christ is Lord. This includes Christ's lordship over the Bible.

To him, then, we turn with our questions about the Bible. How shall we understand biblical authority? How is it used most effectively? How much direct Scriptural quotation is to be employed in our proclamation of the gospel? Is there merit in using the biblical language instead of secular terminology?

The Bible's definition of itself

Jesus' use of Scripture provides clues for answers to each of these questions. But first reference must be made to a phrase most often used by the church in relation to the Bible—"the Word of God." How does the Bible itself use that phrase?

In Genesis we learn that creative power resides in the Word of God (Gen. 1:3). Paul called God's Word "the sword of the Spirit" (Eph. 6:17). Jesus relied on its truths in his temptation struggle (Matt. 4:1-11). Isaiah reminds us of what the Lord said concerning his own Word: "It will not return to me empty, but will accomplish what I desire and achieve the purpose for which I sent it" (Isa. 55:11). It is God's dynamic Word that brings conviction of sin and reveals the promise of pardon (1 John 1:9). Obviously such varied references call for distinctions between the various uses of the phrase "Word of God."

Sometimes "Word of God" is used for what is eternally before—and therefore far bigger than—any book. There was, for example, the dynamic *Word of creation*—"Let there be light," God said, "and there was light" (Gen. 1:3). God's Word called light and life into existence. There is power in such words!

"Word of God" is also used to describe the divinely *revealed message* which came to the prophets of old (Amos 7:16). They were stewards of "the oracles of God." They were to be receptive to its implication, precise in its application, and bold in its proclamation.

The third use of "Word of God" is applied to *Christ himself*. In John 1:1-18, Christ is declared the eternal, personal "Word of God" made flesh. God's Word ("sermon," "mind," "message") becomes incarnate among us, so that by the flesh and blood action of his life, death, and resurrection, he might reveal the heart of God to us.

The church, however, also calls the *Scriptures* the "Word of God." This designation is not inappropriate, for here, under the supervision of the Holy Spirit, we are given a reliable written account of God's acts and their meaning for his people. Interestingly, most of the time when we meet the phrase "Word of God" in Scripture, it does *not* refer to the Bible.

Let us consider, however, what biblical use of the phrase means when it does refer to Scripture. Paul defined a doctrine of inspiration which probably reflected Jesus' own view of Scripture.

All Scripture is God-breathed [inspired] and is useful for teaching, rebuking, correcting, and training in righteousness, so that the man of God may be thoroughly equipped for every good work (2 Tim. 3:16-17).

Careful study of this text shows that the apostolic wording places the emphasis on what divine inspiration achieved, and for what purposes. It avoids perfectionist language, which was foreign to the Hebrew mentality anyway. A word like "flawless," had it been used, would have been meant hyperbolically. If intended literally, it would have incited endless argumentation.

So the chosen (inspired) word was "useful" or "profitable," which can be understood and supported in every Christian life. The purpose of God's inspiration of Scripture was to make it useful in the areas of "teaching," "rebuking," "correcting," and "training in righteousness." This was so "that the child of God may be thoroughly equipped for every good work."

All that is essential for a right relationship with God and with persons, all that is necessary for salvation in its present and future dimensions, is communicated with total reliability through the Old and New Testaments. For this reason we are ready to confess our faith in the Bible as "the word of God and only perfect rule in all matters of faith, doctrine, and practice."[7]

Sadly, there are those in the church who do not accept the full authority of Scripture. They are out of step with their Lord. It is equally sad that many who do profess to accept the authority of Scripture try to improve on Paul's definition of inspiration and insist that it says more than it does. This also is out of step with Jesus.

As Jesus Christ is Lord of the Sabbath, so he is Lord of Scriptures. Because he existed before the book, he ranks above the book, although it bears a truthful witness to him (Luke 24:27). How Christ used Scripture is what we shall be studying in the following pages. We will keep in mind, however, that the phrase, "the Word of God" refers to the dynamic creative Word, the divine and prophetic message, the personal Word incarnate, as well as the inspired Word written (the Bible with its two testaments in our day, the Old Testament in Jesus' day).

Jesus' use of Scripture

It is to the written Word that we now turn. Looking into the four Gospels I have identified most, if not all, of the references Jesus makes to the Old Testament. Analyzing these, I hoped to learn from him how we ought to understand and use the Scriptures in our mission of announcing the good news.

In the Gospel of Matthew, which among the four Gospels places heaviest reliance on the prophetic implications of the Old Testament, we have, as we would expect, the most references by Jesus to the Old Testament. There are approximately fifty-four of these references to the Old Testament. Matthew records Jesus quoting directly from it twenty-four times, and referring to it in a more general way at least thirty times.

In his time of private struggle with temptations and on the cross, Jesus used Scripture four times. He referred to the Old Testament twenty-one times when with the disciples. To the Pharisees, he gave sixteen references and to the crowds, five. Matthew also noted single references to Scripture that Jesus made to the Sadducees, the rich young ruler, the high priest, and John the Baptist.

Mark has at least twenty-three references by Jesus to the Old Testament. Ten are direct and thirteen are indirect. About the same number are directed to the Pharisees as to the disciples. A leper, young ruler, the scribes, priests, and Sadducees also hear Jesus cite Scripture to them.

Luke records thirty-two references by Jesus to the Old Testament. Twelve are direct quotes and twenty indirect. Luke also notes that Jesus used Scripture with the people ten times and with his disciples also about ten times. The polemical use of Scripture is de-emphasized by Luke—he mentions only one instance of its use with the Pharisees, twice with the scribes, and once with the Sadducees, temple merchants, and high priests. John the Baptist is given encouragement by Scripture through his servants, and Jesus' personal devotional use of Scripture is again noted.

John makes reference to Jesus' use of the Old Testament on thirteen occasions, but only five of these could be considered a direct quote. In John, Jesus' use of Scripture is primarily in the area of teaching the people regarding his own messianic claims and challenging the teaching of the Pharisees. With two exceptions, all references are from the Pentateuch or Psalms.

Having identified most (if not all) references Jesus makes to the Old Testament, what can we conclude from a study of this material? And how does Jesus' use of Scripture provide guidelines for our use of the Bible in sharing the good news?

Guidelines for using Scripture

At least five important deductions can be made. First, Jesus knew Scripture. From his numerous quotations, allusions, and more general references to the Old Testament, it is immediately apparent that Jesus was intimately acquainted with the content of his

Scriptures. His knowledge of Scripture is also reflected in his vocabulary and chosen images, even when he is not quoting directly from the text.

Since Jesus spent the first thirty years in a Nazareth carpenter shop—not in a parsonage or theological seminary—his grasp of Scripture is all the more significant. It tells us how highly he rated its importance for his life and ministry.

As those called to represent him, we too ought to know "our book." If it meant so much to Jesus, it should hardly mean less to us. We have the New Testament as well! Healthy churches are Bible-centered. They appreciate the biblical emphasis and provide their people with numerous opportunities for systematic study and hearing of Scripture. To develop a deepening knowledge of Jesus Christ and be able to share him, the study of Scripture is indispensable.

The second thing we notice is that Jesus preferred some books. Looking at the list of books to which he often turned, one soon discovers favorites. Time and again, Jesus reminded his hearers of the Law—the books of Moses, or the Pentateuch—especially Genesis and Deuteronomy. He obviously also loved the Psalms and frequently quoted Isaiah. The minor prophets meant a great deal to him, as his many allusions to them indicate. But of the thirty-nine books of the Old Testament, only twenty-three figure in Jesus' references. Some Scriptures fit the need of the hour better than others.

Such selectivity does not argue for partial inspiration. It does suggest that some parts are more relevant to a particular situation than others. The Bible today is a library of sixty-six books, each having its own subject and particular intention. Its general thematic unity in no way eliminates its vast diversity. Therefore it is understandable that, while we ought to learn the content of the whole Bible, we will probably use certain parts more than others. In evangelism, for instance, those records which point to Christ will receive the major emphasis. The precedent for such selectivity is established by Jesus himself.

Third, we see that the Scriptures became Jesus' weapon in time of temptation. Both Matthew and Luke describe Jesus' use of Scripture in his wilderness ordeal. It is interesting to note that the devil also quoted Scripture to Jesus. This reminds us that a "true word" may be the wrong word for a particular situation. In Jesus' struggle for clarity concerning how he would proceed in his messianic mission, the Word of God from Deuteronomy became his sword of victory against all compromising suggestions. After wrestling with the options, Jesus gained strength and conviction for his messianic role as he relied on the wisdom of the Word of God.

In our task as Jesus' witnesses, we also are faced with numerous options regarding procedures and methodology. Our Lord's example of recourse to Scripture is fully applicable to our situation. The Bible still sheds light on our methods as well as on the message. We too face demonic temptations to compromise the gospel demands or borrow the world's ways to "get people in." Our only sure defense against such demonic sidetracks is sane and balanced understanding and use of the Bible.

Confidence in Scripture grows with its regular application in personal and corporate experience. As it proves itself to be "bread" for the soul, or "light" for the way, or "sword" for the battle, it confirms its own trustworthiness. Then the Christian finds that his or her desire better to understand the Scripture increases. In times of temptation, no word of human wisdom will compare to a promise or directive from the Word of God. To sustain our own spiritual health, as well as for winning the battles in the marketplace, we need to know and trust the wisdom of the Word of God.

The fourth thing we notice is that, for Jesus, the meaning of a passage is more important than verbal precision. Jesus did quote from the Old Testament with verbal accuracy many times, reinforcing the value of Scripture memorization. But he more often expressed the biblical ideas in his own words. In a few cases, we are hard pressed to find the location of a "Scripture says" passage (such as John 7:38)! Apparently precision in quotation was not a high priority in most of Jesus' references to the Old Testament.

When we hear Jesus debating with the Sadducees about the resurrection, we feel the impulse to smile as we hear the casual wording Jesus employed in referring to the passage in Exodus 3. He said, "But in the account of the bush, even Moses showed that the dead rise"(Luke 20:37).

Although the Exodus passage is not about the resurrection, the inference drawn from the name of God is irrefutable. If the eternal Lord is "the God of Abraham, and the God of Isaac, and the God of Jacob," he is most certainly "God of the living and not of the dead." The

Sadducees accepted Moses as authoritative, so the reference had punch. But the simple artless way in which Jesus referred to the story as "the account of the bush," shows that he did not treat the original wording with special reverence.

God's Word is truth, and his truth is always bigger than our wording. Translators understand this better than most of us, as they appreciate how several word arrangements can be used to express the same message. How the idea is worded is determined not only by a concern for precision about the idea, but by that vocabulary choice which best suits the particular audience being addressed at the time.

It was not our Lord's purpose to model exegetical preaching from the Old Testament. What he usually did was lift up the thought or event and freely adapt it to fit the point of his teaching. He did so with total confidence in the divine authority of the reference he was using, but he usually indicated no concern for verbatim accuracy even when beginning with "It is written." Jesus knew that the art of communication calls for different words to different people at different times to effectively get across the same message.

Application of this lesson can heighten our confidence in our own verbal arrangements of the good news. Care in doctrinal precision must remain an ingredient of our "stewardship of the gospel." But once the truth of Christ has become a living part of us, our own prayerfully directed words may convey the meaning of our faith more effectively than a verse from the Bible, especially if it is from an outdated version.

The apostle Paul practiced this. In his sermon to the

Athenians on Mars' Hill, he referred to the great biblical themes of creation and judgment. Acts 17:24 and 25 echo Genesis 1:1-3 and Isaiah 42:5, but the only direct quotation Paul made was from a Greek poet (Aratus of Soli; *Phainomena* 5).

Paul knew the members of his audience and respected them enough to show appreciation for the good in their heritage. He used their heritage as a point of contact and a bridge in communication. Paul wanted to convey a scriptural truth, but in this case, the Holy Spirit led him to communicate that truth by quoting a pagan poet! Paul was free to be led in his verbal witness by the love and light of the Spirit. He was following the pattern of Jesus.

Effective communicators have learned the art of putting the timeless truths of God's Word into the time-related language of their contemporaries. Jesus did this, and his example provides one more reason why "the common people heard him gladly." We too will be heard if we voice the gospel in the vocabulary of our day.

In this regard we do well to remember that Jesus did not speak classical Hebrew. He spoke Aramaic, the common language of his day. With a few brief exceptions, the New Testament writers used the popular rather than classical Greek in their writings. If we follow the example of our Lord and his apostles, we will use contemporary translations of the Bible in our sharing of the good news. We will not burden our hearers with archaic language such as used by the 1611 King James Version.

Sixth, we see that Jesus accepted the divine authority of Scripture in his polemics with the scribes and Pharisees as well as in his instructions to his disciples. "Is it not written in your Law?" he would challenge, then add, "the Scripture cannot be broken" (John 10:34-35). Of those who imprisoned the Sabbath with their rules Jesus asked, "Haven't you read what David did?" (Matt. 12:3). To those who questioned the resurrection he said, "Are you not in error because you do not know the Scriptures or the power of God?" (Mark 12:24). Since his antagonists also claimed to believe in Scripture, Jesus' penetrating responses from their common source of religious authority left them speechless.

Jesus' confidence in the divine authority of Scripture is further illustrated by his attestation of its ultimate fulfillment. He reminded his disciples,

> I have not come to abolish them [the Law and the Prophets] but to fulfill them. I tell you the truth, until heaven and earth disappear, not the smallest letter, not the least stroke of a pen, will by any means disappear from the Law until everything is accomplished (Matt. 5:17-18).

Jesus saw the messianic outline in the Old Testament fulfilled in himself. Jesus told his Emmaus disciples that "everything must be fulfilled that is written about me in the Law of Moses, the Prophets and the Psalms" (Luke 24:44). He further charged these disciples for being "foolish" and "slow of heart" because they fail to believe all that Scriptures had taught regarding the Messiah (Luke 24:25-27).

We face a constant struggle with this same foolishness and heart sluggishness. We swallow all kinds of "stuff" about who the antichrist is, or when Jesus will return, or when the world will end, or what Israel, China, or Russia (pre- and post-Soviet Union!) will do. Yet we are hesitant about studying the Word of God itself, which would enable us to recognize its major themes without getting sidetracked by minor issues.

The Christian has a dependable guide in Scripture. We may proclaim with full confidence the message of God's good news precisely because it is God's, and because the Holy Spirit has inspired the writers of the Bible to provide succeeding generations with a trustworthy witness to it.

That non-Christians may not believe this is irrelevant. They are not required to believe in biblical authority. We call them to meet the living Word in Jesus Christ. Then they will come to trust the written witness. Meanwhile, resisting the temptation of arrogance, we will proclaim the gospel in a tone of joyful certainty in the divine authority of the message he has entrusted to us. The promised miracle is that God will speak through our own uttering of his inspired Word.

A world trembling with anxiety and insecurity, a world assaulted by a cacophony of contradictory voices, desperately needs to hear the clear coherent message of God's Word. Our confidence in the authority of the biblical revelation will help create a climate of faith in the gospel. We needn't be unduly defensive or split hairs over the wording of our doctrine of inspiration.

It is tragic that some churches and denominations have split because one faction says the Bible is "inerrant" and the other calls it "infallible." Jesus used neither word, and I doubt he would waste time arguing the distinctions. He was too busy affirming and applying the word. Instead of spending time defending "inerrancy," we might better share God's good news with our neighbors in deeds and language they can understand. This might be closer to Jesus' own preference.

We need to proclaim and apply the gospel message everywhere. The transforming work of God's living Word will fully attest to the authority of the Word as written. Let's learn to use Jesus' word, Jesus' way!

Reflection

The Inter-Varsity Christian Fellowship, Navigators, and other student organizations encourage their members to have a daily quiet time. This period of approximately ten to thirty minutes, usually in the morning, is to be devoted to the study of Scripture and prayer.

I remember both the joys of observing quiet times and the guilt of missing them. (I confess the ledger was more heavily weighted on the missing side.) That burden was somewhat lifted after my seminary training forced me into the Word more regularly. The weekly discipline of sermon preparation also forced me to study the Bible on a regular basis. Still, there seem to be special blessings reserved for us when we read the inspired accounts primarily for the purpose of hearing what God will say to us personally.

Do we have an established time set apart for the meditation and study of a portion of the Bible? The options will best be determined by our individual schedules (morning, noon, evening, daily, weekly). It's a worthwhile discipline.

Chapter Four

Jesus Makes Us His Advertising

Did Jesus use advertising to spread the gospel? We Americans certainly do. Advertising is one of America's most lucrative businesses. If I have a salable product, I advertise its virtues to get it to the people and get their money back to me. If the product lacks virtue, I wrap it in sensuous appeal and proceed to convince the public it does need this item after all. Service is the justification. Greed is often the motive. The commercial success of radio, TV, and printed advertising is beyond dispute. Businesses would hardly invest the millions of dollars they put into advertising if it didn't pay off.

The question is whether such accepted sales techniques should be used in spreading the gospel. How does one advertise nonsalable commodities such as truthfulness and love? No one will doubt their value or the need to advance their acceptance. But how can commercial practices communicate spiritual values? How can a complex sales organization built to brainwash me into buying what it wants me to buy, pandering to my greed and its own, suddenly be transformed into a messenger of light? The gospel is of a totally different order than a commercial article. How then can it be advertised?

Some may say that the Bible itself encourages us to "advertise." "Go tell it on the mountain!" cried the prophet. "By all means I might win some," said Paul. And Jesus himself spoke of the day "to shout it from the rooftops." So, we are told, advertising that proclaims the gospel with convincing appeal has its place.

Maybe. But there is a difference between bearing witness and advertising. The biblical references support the former. "There is a big difference between selling a product and sharing one's faith. The only one who ever sold Christ, sold him out—for thirty pieces of silver!"[8]

The issue centers on the essence of the gospel message itself. Is there a consistency between medium and message or does the medium dull or deny the message? Marshall McLuhan has demonstrated how the medium is no neutral tool. It participates in the overall message either directly or indirectly. McLuhan speaks of "hot" or "cool" communication. *How* we say something colors and shapes *what* we say. The way we express a concept either clarifies or confuses the issue.

In any kind of advertising, what is said is only part of what is heard. How it is presented—context, setting, style, and manner—all contribute to the content of what is received. The medium may at times completely overshadow the message. Skillful advertising has duped millions into buying products for reasons totally unrelated to or misrepresentative of the product itself.

Sharing the gospel with integrity

The question then remains: what tools or vehicles of advertising may appropriately be used for announcing the gospel and publicizing the church?

In Jesus' day the demons being commanded to leave their victims tried to identify Jesus. He forbade them. Jesus wanted no advertising from demonic agencies. Their references to him, although verbally accurate, would only confuse because of the obvious inconsistency between who they were and who he was. In fact, association with demons was made by Jesus' enemies. "By the prince of demons he is driving out demons," they charged (Mark 3:22). Their jealousy and hostility toward him prompted this absurd and blasphemous accusation. Had Jesus allowed himself to use one word of acknowledgment or endorsement from these demons, the charges against him might have seemed credible.

The message of the church can similarly be confused when identified with demonic elements of our society. The age-old tension of being in but not of the world is one which, with respect to media advertising, the American church has not always handled with theological maturity. We have too easily been swept along by the appeal of successful salesmanship techniques. We have felt it legitimate to apply these principles to advancing the cause of Christ. Is it not enough to say, "If it 'works,' use it"?

Let us remember a cardinal teaching of our faith. It is basic to everything else we believe about people. We affirm that all people are made in the image of God. True, we have fallen and marred "the image," but it is not eradicated. We are still God's special creation, with the theological dignity of being something like our Maker (Psalm 8:5). We have an inherent capacity for worship, intellectual reflection and projection, esthetic creativity, moral evaluation, and the capacity to give ourselves to others in love.

These characteristics of the Creator in the human creature establish the infinite value and dignity of persons. Jesus challenged his hearers with "What can a person give in exchange for his or her soul?" The inferred answer is nothing in all the world can equal the value of one person.

Christians believe this and find it reinforced by the death of Christ for all people. The unique significance of all persons is forever affirmed in the blood of Jesus. God rates us so highly that he gave his only Son for our redemption (John 3:16).

God does not, of course, value us because of our virtue or righteousness which, defiled and lacking, leaves us condemned. Rather, God values us simply because of his love for us. Valued by divine grace, we thereby inherit infinite value. This lofty dignity accorded each person is a tremendously important conviction of our Christian faith.

Techniques which cheapen the gospel

Consider, against this profession of our value, practices we endorse when we apply manipulative techniques to get people to make our desired responses.

Look at some evangelistic preaching. Certainly a level of emotion will be evident in any forthright application of the Word of God to the needs of people. But people were also given minds that are to be informed before important decisions are made. To stimulate emotions in order to stir decisions hardly honors the dignity of persons.

Recently I heard a Christian leader address fellow pastors with a message entitled "Ten Ways to Get People to Come Forward." His desire was to see people converted—but is this how Jesus sends us forth? Are we called to "get people to do" anything? Aside from this leader's first point regarding the need for prayer, he did not root his message in the example of Jesus. He simply offered psychological techniques. His defense would be that "they work."

Without denying that God can work even through our worldly ways, we must look for better ways, methods more in harmony with the style of Jesus himself. John White, associate professor of psychiatry at the University of Manitoba and insightful Christian writer, has noted the techniques some evangelists use to get results. First, he suggests, you make the people anxious by changing the noise levels dramatically—raise and lower the voice or music. Work up "to a crescendo and then let the sound sink into a velvety silence."

Second, induce guilt. Emphasize that someone knows about your sins (God does). Since all people are guilty of something, this is not too difficult to achieve.

Third, destroy ability to make rational judgments. Release the full arsenal of emotional weaponry. A weepy story, followed by indignant assaults against evil, then a joke (a needed relief), and a final "tear jerker" will have wonderful effects. "Before long your experimental rats will have lost touch with all normal bearings by which they know what is what, and you will find that many of them are putty in your hands."[9]

If merely getting converts was the goal of Jesus, could he not have done so in far greater measure than he did? He could have used personal magnetism and spiritual power to get thousands to "come forward." Anyone who could walk unharmed through an angry mob, cause arresting soldiers to fall before him, cleanse the temple of money changers, not to mention all his healings, could certainly have persuaded countless numbers to decide for him. Apparently more was involved than his own skill in getting results. This is a point some of our TV evangelists must ponder. The *restraint* of Jesus has much to teach us in this regard!

Conversions can be produced. Cultists of all varieties use proven techniques to win converts. They get results—but what a denial of biblical faith! Where is the respect for personal sanctity we owe every individual? Where is the honoring of the mind and will of each person? To stir emotions toward an important decision without enlightening rational understanding is an insult to people and a dishonor to the Word of God we are supposedly preaching.

The apostle Paul gives accurate expression to the way of Jesus when he tells the Corinthians,

We have renounced secret and shameful ways; we do not use deception, nor do we distort the word of God. On the contrary, by setting forth the truth plainly we commend ourselves to everyman's conscience in the sight of God" (2 Cor. 4:2).

How commendable are the gimmicks, competitions, and prizes we sometimes use to get people to come to church? What about so-called "Christian graffiti"? Is it any less a desecration of nature or buildings if it reads "Jesus saves" than if it said something else? What about the arrogant competitive boasts appearing in some church advertisements—"the friendliest church," "the most exciting evangelist in America today," "the greatest healer," "the church with the biggest Sunday school"?

Besides cheapening the gospel, these devices reveal an underlying carnality. Their use reflects reliance not on God's Spirit but on human cunning and pride. It assumes that since people can be made to respond like machines, all we need to do is press the right button or pull the right lever to get the desired results. In an age of vast, dehumanizing materialism, it is tragic to see segments of the church fall prey to the same trends. Commercial advertising can so easily snare the church in this sin.

A related subject, of course, is the stewardship among Christians of funds for various publicity purposes. Special services or events need to be brought to the attention of segments of the population; this may call for the use of media advertising. New churches will want to make their presence known, and older churches will want to keep their programs before the people. In this regard, Douglas W. Johnson says, "The general public is most easily reached by mass media. This suggests that spending money for advertisements and announcements is significant."[10]

Significant, yes. But there is no direct correlation between dollars spent and people reached as the article seems to suggest. One church in southern California spends tens of thousands of dollars in commercial advertising. Robert Schuller is crystal clear about his conviction that advertising pays off, and so his church budget always includes a sizable percentage for it. His congregation, formerly Garden Grove Community Church, now the Crystal Cathedral, is growing. There are many laudable things to be noted about its ministry, including the large number of formerly unchurched people who are now members.

But there is another church, Calvary Chapel, not many miles away, that is also growing rapidly. Yet it spends almost nothing on media advertising. I couldn't even find a listing for it in the yellow pages when I visited in 1978. I found the church by asking a garage station attendant. He knew, as do most people in Costa Mesa, where Calvary Chapel is located. A powerful advertising agency was at work—but not of the commercial variety. This church has now parented almost a hundred new churches up and down the state.

The enthusiastic recommendation of happy participants is the best advertising any church can have. Media advertising can supplement but never substitute for the contagious love and enthusiasm of devoted members of Christ's church.

Jesus' use of "advertising"

Let's look now at how Jesus understood and used the advertising possibilities of his day. All four gospels recognize the effectiveness of the witness of John the Baptist. As "front man" for Jesus, his "advertising" power was tremendous. His presence was arresting, his sermons powerful, his message clear. When he pointed to Jesus, his own followers left him for the one whose greatness he acclaimed.

John made no attempt to force anyone to follow Jesus. He simply shared with others the facts about Jesus as he believed them. "Look, the Lamb of God, who takes away the sin of the world!" (John 1:29) he testified. Jesus called John a "burning and shining lamp," and said that "among those born of women there has not risen anyone greater than John the Baptist" (Matt. 11:11). The clear and persuasive announcement of a devoted witness stands squarely in the center of our Lord's advertising policy.

After John's death there was no one to herald Jesus in quite the same way. His apostles were at times sent before him as his representatives. "Whoever receives you receives me," he told them. After Pentecost they became his sole advertisement. To the extent that their pointing to Jesus was clear, they were effective agents of good advertising. That they were fruitful in their witness is evidenced by the phenomenal growth of the early church in an empire that had declared Christianity illegal!

The issue is clarified again—the sincere and enthusiastic testimony of devoted witnesses is the preferred biblical mode for advancing the gospel. It still brings more people to membership in a local church than any other method.

Word of mouth and limited written material were the main "advertising" mediums of Jesus' day. With all the technological advances in media and other avenues of advertising available today, would we not be foolish to ignore the possibilities they afford? No doubt—but too eager an endorsement of them is also foolish, and can be a contradiction of the gospel itself.

Is this not what Jesus recognized so clearly in his temptation experience in the wilderness? It would be great to turn stones into bread, not only for his own need, but to feed the hungry of the world. Since he was able to do it, and cared about the hungry, the temptation was alluring.

But the risk of a suggestion of bribery, and the possibility of leading people to focus on physical needs and thereby missing the deepest needs of their souls, led Jesus to reject this avenue of advancing his messianic mission. It was not an evil method in itself. He did at times miraculously feed the hungry. But this would not accurately represent the message he came to bring, so he rejected it as a demonic suggestion.

A second temptation was to "wow" the crowds with an amazing feat—"throw yourself down" from the pinnacle of the temple and have the angels catch you before you can be hurt (Matthew 4:5-6). A real temptation for one who could achieve it! And why not? It would certainly arrest attention and demonstrate his power.

Once again, Jesus turned aside this suggestion, recognizing its source as from the devil and not God.

Tricks captivate our curiosity but do not lead us to repentance. Tricksters make us gape in amazement but do not lead us to loving allegiance.

Moreover, the person who can pull off colossal feats is not one of us. He is different and apart from us. Jesus came to be among us as one of us, who would need the same caution and protection we need on the heights or in the depths. Jesus would not make the kingdom call a circus spectacle or cloud heaven's values with worldly fanfare.

Finally, the devil pointed out "all the kingdoms of the world" and told Jesus there were methods by which he could reach them all—"in one generation." All he would have to do was compromise a little here and there.

Jesus said, "No!" There was only one course to follow in sharing the message of God's gospel. It was the one thing needful for any Christian in any enterprise. "Worship the Lord your God, and serve him only" (Matt. 4:10).

The best advertisement: being Christ's body

Those who worship God do not degrade his children. They shun all dehumanizing, mechanistic techniques. They refuse to manipulate the choices of others. They don't try to impress, astound, or bribe anyone "for the sake of the gospel." But truly, "for the sake of the gospel," they serve God by serving people in his holy and gracious love.

Malcolm Muggeridge once called television the "fourth great temptation." He imagines the offer being made to Jesus to star in his own new show. He will thus be put on the map and be able almost instantly to launch his career as an evangelist known worldwide. The devil muses, "He'd be crazy to turn it down." But Jesus does. He overcomes the temptation to trade "fantasy and images" for "truth and reality."

Like Quentin Schultze, who tells this story,[11] Muggeridge may have overstated his rejection of television. It can be a tool in God's hands. But its use is full of dangers, not least of which is the tremendous expenditure of funds, which generally flow in only one direction. Keeping the program on the air seems to take precedence over all else. Such may not be the wisest stewardship of the tithes and offerings of God's people, especially in our world of such desperate needs for food, medicine, drug rehabilitation, education.

The simple equation that a product requires commercial publicity if it is to obtain wide acceptance, is contradicted by the history of the church. Consider the growth of the church in areas of the world not cordial to its presence. In Indonesia, Korea, Thailand, Africa, South America, and elsewhere, the growth of the Christian community has been promoted by little or no commercial advertising.

In many of the formerly "Iron Curtain," Eastern European countries, the hostile environment prohibited open advertising (and what is called proselytizing as well). Yet when communism collapsed, a growing church was found in East Germany, Poland, Czechoslovakia, and the former Soviet Union itself. The same is true in China. With the breaking down of the walls between East and West, many have been astonished to find a vibrant and fruitful church in these lands that once were totally restrictive of gospel advertising or proclamation.

The early church provides a striking reminder for us. As an illegal religion for three hundred years, Christianity could hardly advance its cause with much open publicity. Yet within its early centuries, marked by several severe waves of persecution, the faith grew to include over a million souls by 313 C.E. (A.D.)! The personal witness of believers—the integrity of their life together, the joyful confidence of their faith, the undaunted hope they cherished, the unselfish mutual caring they demonstrated—all gave an almost irresistible appeal to their message. The Lord kept adding to their number "daily those who were being saved" (Acts 2:47).

Of course it would be unwise to shun the use of commercial advertising altogether. No doubt there is a place for it in the life and witness of the church. But when it is used, care must be taken to guard the total honesty of what is said or suggested. There must be full respect demonstrated for the minds as well as emotions of people. And the church should stretch for highest quality in format, esthetics, and language without loosing the "common touch."

But media advertising is neither fundamental to church publicity nor mandatory for the church's advance. At best it is a supplemental tool which can render valuable assistance. It is not the central instrument for publicizing the gospel. *Christians are!*

Whether the church makes a greater or lesser impact on its community is finally determined by the authenticity of the commitment professed by those who are called "God's people." What Paul said to the Corinthians is as true today: "You are an open letter about Christ . . . written . . . with the Spirit of the living God. Our message has been engraved, not in stone but in living men and women" (2 Cor. 3:3, Phillips).

Malcolm Muggeridge gives much of the credit for his Christian conversion to Mother Teresa. Her selfless commitment to helping the needy children of India and other lands spoke more clearly of the reality of God's love than any written arguments or advertisements he had ever seen or heard.

The transformed life is God's best advertisement. The church is called the body of Christ. When it looks and acts like Jesus, it commends the faith with integrity. Then it is advertising Jesus' word, Jesus' way.

Reflection

When the man born blind received sight by the healing action of Jesus, he became a classic example of the best kind of advertisement. Questioned about his healing, he replied, "One thing I am sure of . . . I used to be blind; now I can see!" (John 9:25, Phillips).

The verbal witness supported by living evidence is unassailable. A convinced enthusiastic believer will be convincing to others.

Do we offer our communities this kind of advertisement?

Chapter Five

Jesus Gave an Invitation

Jesus called people to himself. In association with him they would discover the full implications of God's good news for them. As his followers we announce this good news and invite people to make a commitment to Christ as Lord and Savior. We do so realizing that "if you confess with your mouth, 'Jesus is Lord,' and believe in your heart that God raised him from the dead, you will be saved" (Rom. 10:9). The call to faith in Christ is extended to all. "Everyone who calls on the name of the Lord will be saved" (Rom. 10:13).

For many, extending an invitation after the message is what distinguishes an evangelistic service from another service. An appeal is made to "accept Christ as Savior" with directions for giving this decision visible expression. New converts are asked to raise their hands, stand, or come forward for prayer during the singing of the invitation hymn. Often the more persons come forward, the more successful the meeting (or the evangelist) is rated. How would Jesus rate it?

Our concern in this chapter is to discover the approach of Jesus in this matter of the invitation. Does our approach match his example?

Some Christians have insisted Jesus was the world's greatest salesman. If the approach of Jesus is compared to what North Americans consider generally accepted sales practices, then this description must also be rejected as unbiblical. Jesus did not come into the world to sell the kingdom of God. He came into the world to serve people and thereby demonstrate the presence of the kingdom of God.

Jesus did not live to get and to gain. He lived to give and to die. When he died it was not a sales triumph—but the greatest offering of all. Mastering effective techniques for getting others to buy our product is a totally different occupation than loving others at all costs. At the end of the day, the salesperson wonders how he or she did. Followers of Jesus will be more concerned about how *they* did—did they experience good news, and was God glorified?

Let us watch our Lord invite people to himself to see what principles we may learn to guide our calling of people to discipleship. We will start in the Gospel of Mark.

How Jesus invites disciples

The first two "invitations" Jesus gives are similarly phrased. "Come, follow me . . . and I will make you fishers of men" (Mark 1:17-20). Those words were appropriately offered to fishermen—Simon and Andrew, James and John. Matthew's call is even briefer. It is simply, "Follow me" (Mark 2:14).

These invitations are a summons to follow, to walk

with Jesus in a relationship of learning and obedience. Each disciple is asked to leave one life orientation for another. There is no promise made at this juncture regarding heavenly reward. Jesus simply offers assurance that, if they put themselves under his influence, he will transform them—make them fishers or finders and gatherers of people. (Remember that the fishing analogies in the Bible are about net fishing, not reel fishing. We are sent on a mission of reconciliation to bring people together. We are not sent to bait and "hook them for Christ!")

The invitation has the authority of a command, for it is the King who issues it. It is a call *to give*, not get. That is, it invites people to give allegiance, not gain benefits. It is an invitation to radical personal involvement with Jesus as Lord, not a syrupy offer of comfortable blessings from a "Santa Claus" Savior.

Juan Carlos Ortiz correctly states that "in recent centuries we have been hearing another gospel—a man-centered human gospel. It is the gospel of the big offer. The gospel of the hot sale. The gospel of the irresistible special deal."[12] Such is far from the call of Christ, which is a summons to surrender all to his lordship.

The nature of Christ's invitation receives fuller amplification in the details provided in Mark 3:14-15. Discipleship is described as having three ingredients.

- The disciples are appointed to be "with him."
- They are sent out "to preach."
- They are given "authority to drive out demons."

Discipleship as apprenticeship

The essence of Christian discipleship is a dynamic

personal relationship with Christ akin to an apprenticeship. Renaissance painters understood the concept of apprenticeship better than many of us today. This excerpt from a letter by Michelangelo's father concerning his thirteen-year-old son conveys the idea well.

> I record this first of April how I, Lodovico . . . bind my son Michelangelo to Domenico and David de Tommaso di Currado for the next three ensuing years, under these conditions and contacts to wit, that the said Michelangelo shall *stay* with the above named masters during this time, to *learn* the art of painting, and to *practice* the same, and to be at the orders of the above named. . . .[13]

The word "disciple" can mean "student" or "pupil." But if this suggests taking a course or attending a class to assimilate information, we miss the point. Apprentices didn't just listen to lectures; they lived with the master. Their role as apprentices was not merely to learn information from a teacher, but to pick up their teacher' style and master a craft through working side by side with a master.

The Christian, as a disciple, is called to emulate the style of Jesus. The Christian is to adopt Jesus' priorities and methods until intimate association with Jesus makes the Christian a "Jesus person." The mark of the Master is unmistakably imprinted on the Christian's total life. It was so with the disciples, Peter and John, of whom it was said, "they took note that these men had been *with Jesus*" (Acts 4:13; emphasis added).

The evangelistic invitation is a call to surrender independent control to Jesus, thereby acknowledging his authority to direct one's life. The issue is one of loyalty. It is a summons to recognize and endorse Christ as Lord of our lives. Persons then surrender to Jesus' sphere of influence. They are "with him," and Jesus now makes the fundamental difference in life's decisions.

Discipleship as "going out" for Jesus

The second role in discipleship is to go out for Jesus, to represent him in proclamation of his good news to our world. Good ideas may come by intuition, but good news concerns events. Such news must be reported to be known. What we learn about God's kingdom in Christ is news so good it must be shared or the world is left bereft. The invitation to "follow" means both learning to know Christ and sharing his grace with others.

The evangelistic mission of the church is clearly established, even at this early stage in Christ's ministry. Good deeds will inevitably be central in the church's mission. But the "news" part will call for the use of words. Every congregation of the Christian church has this "word" assignment: "We've a story to tell to the nations."

Being gifted variously within the body of Christ, Christians will exhibit difference in ability to verbalize and share their faith. Some church growth researchers claim that about 8 to 10 percent of the membership in an average size congregation in America has an evangelistic gift. This would imply the capacity (a spiritual gift which is being developed) to present the gospel clearly and convincingly. Others say at least 25 percent are able to be involved in a less frontal "friendship evangelism," which still calls for a measure of articulation.[14]

At a simpler level, it is my conviction that anyone who has ever shared a joyful event with another person has ability to give a verbal witness. If you have shared the news of your promotion, the birth of your child, your wedding announcement, or your graduation, you can tell of God's gracious dealings with you. "Let the redeemed of the Lord say this" (Psalm 107:2) sang the psalmist years ago. The need to speak out remains equally strong today.

Any person who has experienced God's forgiveness and guidance can surely say to another, "I feel grateful to God for his mercy and protection," or "I believe God really cares about us and has some special purpose for each one of us. For me it is. . . ."

When Ann Kiemel was asked what made her so happy, she replied, "Sir, my name is Ann. Do you really want to know? You see I'm a Christian and Jesus is the Lord of my life. He laughs with me and cries with me, and walks lonely roads with me. And sir, he and I are out to change the world. And sir, he can change your world."[15]

Maybe only 10 to 25 percent of any congregation's members are particularly gifted clarifiers of the faith (would that there were that many in each of our churches!). But *all* the regenerative members of a church ought to be able to give some verbal expression of what faith in the Lord implies in daily life. They should be able to share the meaning of their faith not only with the pastor or board of deacons upon joining the church, but in the marketplace—where we are called both to be and to announce "good news."

An indispensable part of discipleship is being sent out "to proclaim the Gospel" (Mark 3:14, NEB). That assignment belongs to all of us. There can be no harvest without first sowing the seed. We are all involved in sowing. This is accepted by many of the growing churches in South America. Believers are instructed to be aggressive witnesses, whether they have the gift of evangelist or not, reports C. Peter Wagner in *Spiritual Power and Church Growth*.

Discipleship and authority over demons

The third ingredient of discipleship mentioned in Mark 3:14-15 is authority over demonic powers. Disciples of Jesus are called to offensive spiritual warfare. It is not enough for Christians to sit home smugly, singing "Safe Am I." Demonic powers are enslaving people in prejudice, greed, addictions, idolatry, deceit, and guilt. Christ imparts to his disciples the resurrection potential of new life which liberates from these demonic chains. In this sense Christians are called to be exorcists. They exercise this authority in Jesus' name and on his behalf.

When the seventy disciples returned from a mission, they reported the redeeming power of Jesus' name over the demons. Jesus said, "I saw Satan fall like lightning from heaven" (Luke 10:18). Whenever Christians enable others to enthrone Christ, Satan falls. Whenever the ways of Christ prevail over the ways of the world, Satan falls again.

We are called to exalt Christ. In so doing, we bring the devil down. When we trust Christ as Lord, wonderful reconciliations among people happen, and marvelous healings do occur. The grip of the evil one breaks.

Disclosing the cost of discipleship

The full implications of what it means to follow Jesus cannot be given each time the gospel invitation is extended. But biblical integrity requires that hearers be told the cost of loyalty. It may come as a surprise to many, but the Bible does not record invitations to "accept Jesus as Savior." Instead, people are regularly invited to acknowledge Jesus as Lord. The invitation is not a free offer of heaven's blessings. It is a call to commitment—to be with Jesus, to go out and speak for him, and to be involved in his war against the demonic forces in life.

Reading on in Mark's account, we see the definition of discipleship sharpened even further.

> Then he called the crowd to him along with his disciples and said: "If anyone would come after me, he must deny himself and take up his cross and follow me. For whoever wants to save his life will lose it, but whoever loses his life for me and for the gospel will save it" (Mark 8:34-35).

The cost and conditions of following Jesus are stated. It is no easy ride. It is not a popular course. It may generate conflict among those nearest you.

> "If anyone comes to me and does not hate his father and mother, his wife and children, his brothers and sisters—yes, even his own life—he cannot be my disciple.

And anyone who does not carry his cross and follow me cannot be my disciple" (Luke 14:26-27).

Instead of fanning the flames of the crowds' devotion, Jesus seems to pour on cold water. The crowds stop in their tracks, amazed. So do we. Is not Jesus the one who teaches a love so expansive it includes even our enemies? What could he possibly mean by "hating" our nearest and dearest? Helmut Thielicke suggests that the word "hate" was hyperbole chosen for its "siren"[16] effect. It is a warning to stop, look, listen! It forces us to ask, "What does this mean"?

A college friend of mine discovered what Jesus meant even before he read this text. Through the witness of friends in the Inter-Varsity chapter at the University of Winnipeg, Lou became a Christian.

When on Sunday he told his parents he was going to a church nearby, his father exploded. The gist of his comments was, "Lou, have I not taught you better? Did I not tell you what this religion did to the poor in the old country—how the church and the rich exploited the peasants?

"Besides, it is all a lot of superstition. I thought you had more respect for your father's instruction than to be duped by those religionists."

Lou tried to explain his newfound faith, but to no avail. The following week, he reported to us that his father had said, "If you persist in this religious garbage you don't love me!"

With deep emotion, Lou told his classmates, "My dad thinks I hate him."

To place Jesus above the wishes of those closest to

us may indeed seem a "put-down" of them. But Christ's call is clear. He is Lord and that means position number one. We may come to him with all kinds of expectations, but here he demands that we recognize his expectations of us. If we are not prepared to enthrone him, we are not prepared for discipleship.

The strictness of this requirement is later recognized to be a call of infinite grace. It is for our ultimate happiness that the demand is so stringent. For it is in the single-mindedness of complete allegiance that the joy of following is realized. The order of the prayer of St. Francis is correct: "It is in giving that we receive; it is in dying that we are born to life eternal."

The temptation of modern evangelism is to bait the audience with the promise of blessings instead of clarifying the true path by which they are reached. The result has been the enormous percentage of dropouts from the numbers of decisions made in evangelistic campaigns. Would such be the case if we were faithfully spelling out the costs of discipleship?

The cost of discipleship, as Jesus described it, is bearing a cross. The cross was an instrument of death. Plainly stated, Jesus calls us to die. Our former orientation with its loyalties and affections must die. The new he promises is so radically different, it leaves the old in a grave. The new has about it the flavor of Jesus' resurrection. So the way of the cross becomes the way to life. Life is saved only when one's own way is "crossed out" in favor of Jesus' way. Those who lose their lives are the ones who find it, and what they find is indescribably abundant.

Jesus loves us too much to hide his conditions in

fine print. Enthusiastic starters are fine, but Jesus wants us to finish the course as well. His invitations tell the truth about the Christian pilgrimage. They warn us about what is involved. Jesus does not intend to frighten us away from making a decision for him. He is not saying, "If you fear you may fail don't start!" Rather, he is preparing us for what is actually included in our discipleship-relationship with him. He lets us know there is a cost to be paid. Then he enables us, by his strength, to pay it. And so we begin with full reliance on his power.

The most poignant illustration of Jesus' honesty in extending the discipleship invitation is recorded in Mark 10. There we meet the rich young man who asks Jesus what he must do "to inherit eternal life." Jesus points him to the commandments, which he sincerely believes he has kept. Jesus, Mark tells us, "loved him," not simply with the love Jesus has for all persons, but with a special admiration for his idealism.

Then Jesus points out the one additional thing the rich man must do. "Go, sell everything you have and give to the poor, and you will have treasure in heaven. Then come, follow me" (Mark 10:21).

Mark records that the young man's "face fell. He went away sad, because he had great wealth" (Mark 10:22).

Doesn't it seem amazing that, after we are told Jesus really loved this man, he would let him go so easily? There is not a hint of any attempt to change the young man's mind. There is no following after him, no asking him to reconsider, no changing the amount he should give away, no pressure at all. Jesus let him go as completely as the father let his younger son go to the far country when he demanded to leave home (Luke 15:12).

What is the lesson for us here? Does it not challenge our repeated pleadings for decisions ("Let us sing one more verse")? Invitations have their place; the gospel calls for a verdict. But from Jesus we get the model of one who graciously states the nature and conditions of the call with honest disclosure of its cost. He will not have anyone join the discipleship band without knowing the "fine print." Jesus never pushed, tricked, deceived, or pressured anyone into following him.

Have we, at times, been guilty of promising things other than Jesus did? What of suggestions that if we follow Jesus we will be more successful or wealthy? What of appeals to send money and God will make us richer? Would that have been the case for the rich young ruler?

Not according to Jesus. The promises which accompany our Lord's invitations have to do with a cross and what he will make of us when we commit our lives to him.

It should be clear by now that if we follow the pattern of Jesus we will never manipulate people into accepting him. Floyd McClung says,

First, we must never pressure people to accept Christ. We must wait until the people we are ministering to have sufficient understanding of the gospel. They must understand the implications of becoming a Christian. That includes the cost of discipleship. We cannot present the Christian life as a panacea for all ills, or the beginning of a new life of material abundance. . . . Secondly, we must do more than wait for a full understanding of the gospel and its implications. We must also wait for conviction and full repentance. Becoming a follower of Jesus is not just giving mental assent to him. . . . It means giving our whole life over to the lordship of Christ.[17]

We may not be ready to wait for a *full* understanding of the gospel's implications, but certainly some minimal biblical teaching about discipleship must precede the call to commitment. Faithfulness to Christ and integrity with people demand no less. He called people not to give him an hour or two every Sunday. He called people to give him their lives. Any invitation that does less is not communicating Jesus' word, Jesus' way.

Reflection

What do you think of the following invitation?

"Now, with every eye open, everyone looking around, no music in the background, in this awkward moment of silence—if you are ready to commit your life to Jesus as your Lord and Savior—stand and be counted!"

I have used such an invitation on several occasions and found that when a response is made to a clearly defined invitation to follow Christ as Lord, the decision is a serious one and the dropout rate minimal.

Do we use the approach of Jesus in our church service invitations and personal evangelizing?

Chapter Six

Jesus Felt a Sense of Urgency

For Jesus, kingdom concerns were urgent. With eternal consequences at stake, how could anyone view God's work with indifference? Jesus' style was resolute and determined.

For the Christian, the gospel contains an imperative that springs from the necessity of love. Paul spoke of the love of Christ "constraining" him. The New English Bible words it like this: "for the love of Christ leaves us no choice" (2 Cor. 5:14, NEB). This was Paul's motivation in persuading people. The same was true for the other apostles. They proclaimed the gospel with a zeal and commitment that clearly evidenced their high sense of mission.

This impelling motive sprang from their worship of God and relationship with Jesus. He was God's news, news too good to hide, so they heralded him among all people. The great commission made it clear that, wherever they went, they were to be about the task of "disciple making" (Matt. 28:19). No news was better; therefore, no assignment was more imperative.

However, this sense of urgency was not a frenzied rush. The distinction is important. We understandably hesitate to note that Jesus did not press the salvation message on everyone he met. Christians are often so reluctant to share the gospel that we fear saying anything which might excuse lack of evangelistic zeal.

I remember with a smile what D. L. Moody once said about his critics. "I like my way of doing it better than their way of not doing it." Yet the dangers of the "rush job" are serious. The pressure tactics of some have boomeranged, causing other Christians greater hesitancy in openly sharing the gospel.

Jesus' model of urgency

How does Jesus model the urgency that befits the messenger of his kingdom?

The thirty years of Jesus' preparation in Nazareth cannot be forced into meaning that we should not begin to speak until we have put in an equivalent period of preparation. Yet Jesus' preparation time is important to consider (as explored in chapter 5). How do we square his concern for the lost with his remaining in the carpenter shop until age thirty?

There was the need for appropriate preparation before launching on a public ministry. Jesus' preparation was not formal, but a full immersion into the common life of people. His spiritual preparation followed the normal channels open to anyone in his town—the synagogue, Scriptures, yearly temple visits, devotions, sensitivity to the presence of God everywhere. As far as we know, Jesus' preparation included no special opportunities—except the privilege of a godly home. Even God would not risk bringing his Son into the world in a faithless home!

So Jesus' period of preparation was in the routine world of people—working and playing, marrying and burying, worshiping and studying, succeeding and failing. He learned to know people. By listening to them he learned what it took to love them.

When he finally emerged from obscurity to herald the kingdom of God, he began with an act of identification with sinners. He was baptized by John with a "baptism of repentance." He was one of us!

Whatever other preparation is needed, this is vital: knowledge and love of people marked by full identification with their joys and sorrows.

Another lesson we may take from this silent period of Jesus' life is that it demonstrates sublime confidence in the providence of God. The timing of the heavenly Father was trusted by Jesus. Floyd McClung, commenting on Jesus' years in the carpenter shop, says,

> It tells me that God does not have the same huge sense of urgency that we've got. Our false sense of urgency does a great deal of harm to the gospel. Jesus was a friend of sinners. He was available to them. He was willing to spend time with them. He didn't have to "win them" now.[18]

To say we don't have to win people now sounds almost heretical to evangelical ears. Yet is this not the pattern of Jesus? How often did he heal and help people without a word from Scripture or any reference to how they could be saved? Most of the time!

Jesus came among us to serve. This meant meeting people where they were and addressing the needs most pressing at the time. It could be forgiveness of sin, as with the paralytic (Mark 2:5) or healing a withered hand (Mark 3:5). The man whose hand was healed received no tract or decision card.

It is dangerous to argue from silence, but there are too many references in Jesus' ministry to good deeds without words for us to miss the point. The good news may at times be feeding the hungry, sheltering the weak, healing the sick, welcoming the strangers—and that may be sufficient for the moment.

No one act includes everything contained in the gospel (nor does any one tract). But free from the pressure of having "to win them now," Jesus simply loved persons and entrusted them to the care of the Father's good will and perfect timing for their lives.

Tomorrow would provide another occasion in which the people could experience the grace of God and take another step of faith. Each new day would bring, besides trials, its own set of opportunities for growth in trust and obedience to the will of God. Everything did not have to be settled in one day.

Jesus never exhorted his disciples to get to their neighbors fast, before disease or a Roman sword caused their death. The evangelistic appeal, "be saved tonight, you may never see tomorrow!" is a dangerous half-truth. Of course we cannot know when death may strike. But neither can we fully determine when a particular individual is ready to make an intelligent commitment to Christ.

Today may or may not be a person's day of salvation. There are growth needs prior to a mature decision, even as there are growth needs afterward. Persons ought not step ahead of where they should be, nor should we so encourage them. Bishop Festo Kivengere from Uganda says,

> You Americans are always counting. You think your meetings are not successful unless you can count large numbers of converts. This puts you in danger of plucking unripe fruit! Let God ripen the fruit in his good time and then the harvest will come easily and naturally.[19]

Maybe some of our more fervent altar calls are really piously disguised lack of faith! Why are we always asking to see results? Do we not believe God honors the faithful proclamation of his Word? Where is our reliance on the ministry of the Holy Spirit? Maybe Jesus still sighs regarding some of us, "Oh you of little faith."

I am reminded of a lonely person whom I met on Colorado Avenue in Pasadena. Wearied of Hebrew studies, I had taken a walk to refresh myself, then I encountered this man. He asked if I had any change. I hesitated, then explained I was about to leave school for lack of funds. I did offer him my company if he was open to a little conversation for a few blocks.

He accepted and surprised me by his openness. Our sharing became more comfortable, so we stopped for coffee. When I offered to get him a room at the local YMCA, he refused, because it would cost me too much. He knew of a less expensive place.

I accompanied him to a flophouse and discovered where many of the homeless live. There were about six men on mattresses on the floor in the shabbiest of conditions. The cost was $2.00 a bed.

There was a Gideon Bible on a wooden box. I asked if I might share a verse or two with him. He eagerly accepted. I read about the Good Shepherd and offered a few sentences of prayer.

Before we parted he said something which left a lasting impression.

"You remind me," he said, "of a guy I met in Texas."

When I asked in what way, he told me about a person who had to have been a Christian.

I realized God was using me as one of many links in the chain of events the Spirit intended for this person. I was not the first nor the last of God's witnesses who would play a role in his life.

A great peace came over me as I realized that the whole burden of this man's salvation was not mine to carry. I was to be faithful with each opportunity as God ordained. No more, no less, is required. This "stranger-become-friend" had made an important contribution to my life. He had taught me a new appreciation of God's sovereignty!

Jesus completely trusted the Father's timing and the Spirit's guidance concerning when and what he should say or do to meet the needs of those he met. His tempo should be ours.

Jesus seems not to have allowed the pressure of supposed deadlines to prevent his meeting immediate needs. When en route to the home of Jairus, a woman reached out and touched him for healing. Jesus stopped to inquire who it was.

At the same time, the daughter of Jairus "was dying"

(Luke 8:42), so Jesus was on an urgent mission. Yet Jesus stopped along the way to identify and bless an unnamed woman.

We sense the anxiety of Peter and the others when Jesus paused to inquire who touched him. Peter said, "You see the people crowding against you . . . and yet you can ask, 'Who touched me?' " (Mark 5:31). Peter implied Jesus' question was foolish, for many had touched him. Moreover, Jairus was an important man, a ruler of the synagogue, and he needed Jesus now! "Let's move!" was Peter's unspoken wish.

But our Lord's pace was right. There was time for the unnamed woman and there was time for Jairus' daughter. The greater glory came to God when he raised her from death later that day (Mark 5:42).

Jesus' model of rest

Jesus knew how to pace himself. He didn't waste time, nor did he rush. He also knew the value of retreats. When the pressures of the crowds mounted, he said to his disciples, "Come with me by yourselves to a quiet place and get some rest" (Mark 6:31).

We read of other occasions in which Jesus retreated for refreshment and rest when conflict became heavy. Apparently he did not consider it cowardly or escapist to do this. Once he went to the coastlands of Phoenicia and on another occasion to the headwaters of the Jordan at Caesarea Philippi, where the air is cooler and the terrain greener than in the more arid south. Isn't it interesting that we read of three specific times of retreat or vacation during his three years of ministry?

What does this say to the workaholic or the minister

who piously refuses to take a vacation because there is too much to do? Why do we try to go one better than Jesus? Isn't he our true way? He should be our example in this matter of pacing and timing as well.

Our Lord had the biggest job any person has ever had to accomplish. He did it without nervously tearing around. He did it by caring about the people he met, in the sublime confidence that each day lived in the light of his Father's direction was to the glory of God—and therefore entirely satisfactory.

After such a day he could sleep, even in the stern of a boat in the midst of a storm (Mark 4:38). With such a balance of work and rest, Jesus could, when the time was right, set his face "like a flint" to move with strength into the most difficult battles before him. What a great example for this stress-torn generation!

Paul urges us to "never be lacking in zeal, but keep your spiritual fervor" (Rom. 12:11). But this does not imply ceaseless activity. The glow will remain longer in the faces of us who, like our Lord, are nourished in pastures that are both inward and outward. We will "come in and go out, and find pasture" (John 10:9).

Whether the lesson be drawn from the silent or active years of Jesus' ministry, the point is that because our Lord trusted the timing of God, neither was he in a rush himself, nor did he hurry others. Both his worship of God and respect for people allowed for no other approach. We stand convicted of a need for greater faith in the wisdom and timing of our sovereign God. Let our sense of urgency be like that of Jesus.

Of course, to use Jesus' model of rest to justify lack of zeal in sharing the gospel misses the point. Resting as Jesus did has a liberating potential. The example of Jesus sets us free from the false guilt of failure to meet needless deadlines. Then we can be led by the timing of God's Spirit in sharing the gospel. Then we can also leave the results of our sharing with the Holy Spirit, who alone does the convicting and regenerative work in people's lives.

We shall also be able to laugh along the way. There are so many happy incongruities in life to chuckle over. If Jesus could smile and make humorous comments, maybe we need to take time for the same. A cheerful spirit is still great medicine. And joyful Christians are still the most effective witnesses.

Being in tune with Jesus' style of urgency will free us to walk among people as God's good news. We shall impart his love to them in ways that respect who they are, where they are, and what their needs are at the moment. Such sensitivity demonstrates a sharing of Jesus' word, Jesus' way.

Reflection

Busyness rapes relationships . . . it fills a calendar but fractures a family. It cultivates a program but plows under priorities. . . . In place of quiet, responsive spirit we offer Him an inner washing machine—churning with anxiety, clogged with too much activity and spilling over resentment and impatience. Sometimes He must watch our convulsions with a heavy sigh.[20]

Ponder the difference between pressured activity and the sense of divine urgency in our mission.

Chapter Seven

Jesus Understood About Heaven and Hell

Jesus brought good news for today and for tomorrow. Heaven and hell are about both today and tomorrow. Jesus referred to each many times. If we are sharing his word faithfully, we must include his understanding of heaven and hell.

Death is life's great enigma. We want to live, but we all die. We don't like it. Separation from loved ones tears the heart; the stench of corruption turns the stomach. The finality of death shocks the mind, although it is the most common fact of existence. After the shockwaves of death have convulsed us, we ask the inevitable question, "Is that all there is to life?" Is there possibly something more, some continuation of life in a new form? "If a man dies, will he live again?" (Job 14:14).

Jesus gives an emphatic "yes" to this question. The way he handled his own death is one of the most radically new ingredients of the gospel. For Jesus death was a moment of intense crisis and terrible solitude. But his death marked a completion, not a finality.

Death became a doorway through which Jesus passed to a new beginning! His resurrection dramatically signaled the defeat of death's powers. The grave had lost its inexorable grip. The resurrection of Christ sings the song of hope, of new and deathless life, of the victory of love and justice over hate and injustice.

As Peter proclaimed, "God raised him from the dead, freeing him from the agony of death, because it was impossible for death to keep its hold on him" (Acts 2:24). So Easter becomes the Christian's most joyful festival. In fact, each Lord's Day is a celebration of his resurrection!

The next question has to do with who shares in the resurrection victory of Christ. Do all people participate in this blessed hope? If they do not now, will they ultimately? If what we do in this life has anything to do with the afterlife, this is a crucial matter and a vital ingredient of Christian proclamation. Again we turn for guidance to our Lord.

It does not take long to discover that Jesus does refer to life beyond the grave. Furthermore, his teachings lead us to the sobering conviction that two possible destinies await us after death. The traditional identification of these is *heaven* and *hell*.

With those alternatives in mind, I felt as a young Christian that I ought to remind others of the ultimate consequences of our actions. I was soon puzzled by how little weight the argument seemed to carry. I shall never forget the response I received from an artist friend, almost four times my senior.

When I seemed to be running short of arguments for my faith I said, thinking I was playing my trump card, "Well, Mrs. Warren, don't you want to go to heaven when you die?"

Her reply was emphatic, "Certainly not!"

Stunned, I meekly inquired about why.

She continued, "I have no interest in wearing a kimono, playing a harp, and sitting around singing for ever and ever!"

Then after a pause she sighed, "When we die, we die and that's it."

I was certain that was not "it," but the force of her response affected me like three fastballs—against which I had struck out.

I have had trouble with hell, but I didn't expect anyone could have trouble with heaven. I soon realized we know very little about what these words mean. And much of what we have said has made the situation worse, not better.

Few Christian teachings have been more maligned and caricatured than our faith in heaven, which is often viewed as unsophisticated or presumptuous. The way some Christians have preached and written about heaven has justifiably invited criticism. Others scorn thoughts about heaven as "pie in the sky, bye and bye." As for ideas of hell, these are considered archaic at best and barbaric at worst. If heaven seems pale, hell seems intolerable.

So we tend to ignore these concepts or skip over

them when we find them in the Bible. In most churches there is little preaching about heaven or hell.

When asked to preach on one occasion, the former publisher Frank Sheed wrote, "I seized the opportunity to give a sermon on Heaven, so that I should not die without ever having heard one." Alfred C. Krass gives us this choice quote and adds, "I cannot recall that I have ever heard one either."[21]

A faithful proclaimer of the gospel cannot avoid the issue of our afterlife destiny. What does the New Testament say about it? People want to know, and so evangelists have usually been in the forefront of those who preach about heaven and hell.

Unfortunately, much of the caricature and misrepresentation can also be traced to these sources. The scholarly preacher of America's second Great Awakening, Jonathan Edwards, preached a powerful sermon called, "Sinners in the Hands of an Angry God." It was far more balanced than the title suggests to modern ears. However, that portrayal has left this indelible impression: God holds us over a burning abyss, and if we do not say or do the right thing he will drop us in!

I heard one evangelist tell his audience, "I personally don't care if you go to heaven or hell. I'm just here to tell you that you're headed for one or the other." If he cared that little, I didn't care to listen to him. I felt a surge of compassion for those in the congregation subjected to such heartless bombast.

D. L. Moody was much closer to the heart of our Lord when he testified that he could not speak about hell without tears in his eyes. Those who heard him acknowledged this to be true. Wesley Nelson once said that the idea of hell does not just "drive one to tears; it drives one to insanity!"

There are Christians who feel that their motive for witness must be to save people from hell. They remember the picture of millions of heathen walking blindly over a precipice to fall into eternal damnation because they had never heard the name of Jesus. So with genuine compassion (and often with some paternalism), they go to the "heathen" with the message of rescue—only to find the heathen do not want rescue!

The "rescue from hell" motif does not appear to drive Jesus' ministry. It is there, but not as the fire of his motivation. Our missionaries and evangelists should thus see it as an inferior motive as well.

Jesus' teachings on heaven and hell

What did Jesus believe and teach about heaven and hell? Some biblical references to these themes refer to consequences received in this present life. There is a "heaven" or "hell" to be experienced by all of us in our lifetime on this planet. This is how some biblical scholars interpret most references to heaven or hell in the Sermon on the Mount (Matt. 5—7).

However, when Jesus speaks of a final "day of judgment" (Matt. 10:15; 11:24; 12:36) he states that after death closes our earthly journey, we will still have to stand before our Maker for his verdict. And the verdict will determine something that follows. Jesus warns, "Do not be afraid of those who kill the body but cannot kill the soul. Rather, be afraid of the One who can destroy both soul and body in hell" (Matt. 10:28). These words point to a dramatic consequence which follows this life.

Jesus' parables on the stewardship of talents (Matt. 25:14-30), the separation of sheep from goats (Matt. 25:31-46), and the rich man and Lazarus (Luke 16:19-31) also illustrate an ultimate divine judgment that follows this life. Jesus speaks of those who "did not do for one of the least of these, you did not do for me. Then they will go away to eternal punishment, but the righteous to eternal life" (Matt. 25:45-46). These words affirm a last judgment based on God's estimate of our faithfulness in this life.

There can be no question about the contemporary "daily life" emphasis of Jesus' teaching as reported in the four Gospels. His stress is on the present life, lived out in obedient relationship to God, with ethical implications in relationship with others. While it is not primarily about the future, the message of Jesus includes, as an indispensable element, a final judgment.

The theme of heaven is an inseparable adjunct to the teaching on hell. No geographic or architectural details about either "place" or "state" are offered by Jesus. But he uses bold and vivid imagery. "Lake of fire" and "outer darkness" would exclude each other if taken literally. However, they are powerful figures of hell's judgment and alienation from the presence of God.

The language of heaven includes "eternal life" (Mark 10:30; John 3:16), "your master's happiness," (Matt. 25:21) "never perish" (John 10:28), "my Father's house" (John 14:2, 23), and the "new Jerusalem" (Rev. 21:2). Resurrection morning finds "the saved" ushered into life in its fullest and most beautiful dimensions. There the presence of God is the joyful light on every new adventure of work and worship.

Jesus teaches us that life on this planet is not everything there is. Some of our decisions during this lifetime have eternal ramifications. Our ultimate destiny, as with our present life, is determined by the presence or absence of God in our life. To acknowledge God's presence as Lord opens the door to heaven. To deny God is to choose hell. This, I believe, is the teaching of Jesus.

Our experience of heaven and hell

Before we dismiss this teaching as accommodation to his generation's worldview, let us examine our own experience. Have we not sampled something of heaven and hell already? We know well that there is a direct relationship between our actions and their consequences. In a journey, direction determines destination. In gardening, seed determines harvest. So in most of life, our choices determine the outcome.

If this is how our world operates, is it reasonable to suggest that the God who created both this world and the next, would contradict those principles for the next world? Such a possibility receives no support from the Bible. Does not the fact of judgment every day provide a fundamental clue to a final judgment day?

My personal experience helps me understand heaven and hell, both now and later. I have suffered the agony of regret; I have also been exhilarated by the inspiration of hope. I have felt the pangs of guilt; I have also enjoyed the wonder of pardon. I know the pain of alienation; I also know the bliss of reconciliation. I know both hell and heaven, for I have experienced their reality already.

Does this life then provide hints about the next? The inspired writers believed so. The apostle Paul wrote,

> Do not be deceived: God cannot be mocked. A man reaps what he sows. The one who sows to please his sinful nature, from that nature will reap destruction; the one who sows to please the Spirit, from the Spirit will reap eternal life (Gal. 6:7-8).

The harvest principle is as certain in the moral realm as in the field of agriculture. As wheat seed produces wheat and weed seed produces weeds, so hate seeds produce hate, and love gives birth to love.

Sin often leads us into trying an end run around this principle. We cheat and lie yet still hope to reap a harvest of trust and peace. Deception may prevail for a moment. But it does not stand the test of time, much less the test of eternity. Sooner or later we reap what we sow. The sad element in this spiritual law of the harvest is that since we have all "sown to please the sinful nature," we are all infected by and headed towards destruction.

The good news of the gospel

Exactly here the story of Jesus becomes good news. On the cross, Christ's self-giving overcame our self-seeking. His sowing of love was greater than our plantings of sin. He carried the full load of our hellish harvest and deposited it in a tomb. Because he included us in his resurrection, we are invited to share in the harvest of his planting. He planted a life of complete obedience to the will of the Father, so its fruit would be a family of daughters and sons living in harmony with the Father's will.

In Christ we can stand before the Almighty Judge, pardoned, accepted, and unafraid. In Christ, we have learned to sow "to please the Spirit" and so reap "eternal life" (Gal. 6:8).

The biblical message on heaven and hell is a reminder that God has created a world in which orderly laws operate. Our experience stands in full conformity with the Word of God. We actually know a great deal about heaven and hell. Our problems usually lie in trying to reach heaven via a hellish route. We still want the good results while excusing our evil ways.

The cross is God's "stop sign" along this self-centered way. The Calvary portrayal of innocent suffering tells the story of sin's harvest. Sin kills the best there is! God's warning regarding hell is evidence of his love. "Stop!" God calls to us. Don't go the way of death, "choose life, so that you and your children may live" (Deut. 30:19).

God does not renege on his promise of personal freedom to each of us. We might say that he takes responsibility *toward* but not *for* us. God has provided the way of salvation for us but does not force us into that way. We are not pressured against our will into either heaven or hell.

God wants us to share the peace and joy of his presence. Bethlehem, Golgatha, and Calvary describe the extent and intensity of God's desire for our wholeness, well-being, and eternal life. God's appeal to sinners is a loving call to come to him for this gift of life abundant and eternal. To accept his invitation is heaven; to refuse it is hell.

Declaring the good news

Evangelists are responsible to speak clearly to this issue. Love makes them messengers of warning. The logic of heaven and hell is as firm as the rock of Gibraltar. Although free to choose many things, we are not free to choose the outcome! Love calls for making the wisest choices and urging others to do the same. To refuse to warn people is not merely a failure in theology, it is a failure of love.

If you know the bridge is washed out along the road ahead, do you not stop your vehicle and wave down approaching traffic? "Don't go that way!" you cry out. Those who heed your cry will be grateful. Those who ignore it will suffer the tragic consequences. God has posted his cross-shaped stop sign along the way to disaster. We ignore it to our peril!

Clarity in the preaching of ultimate destiny calls for a forthright declaration of the good news. There is a way to life eternal! This is the way God has made for all the world in Jesus Christ. "Salvation is found in no one else, for there is no other name under heaven given to men by which we must be saved" (Acts 4:12). The resurrection of Jesus validated his testimony to be the true and living way to God (John 14:6).

Only God's way saves

But this affirmation is not the same as what is sometimes heard from those who assert that their brand of religion is the best or only way to God. It is God's way that saves, not ours. There are enough evidences of the presence of Jesus Christ in many others to give us pause before consigning them to hell simply because they may not share our particular experience of Christ, denomination, or vocabulary of Christian testimony.

The New Testament affirms that no one comes to God except through Jesus Christ. It does not, however, insist that all share an identical experience of Christ. All persons are called simply to repent and trust the mercy of God. "Everyone who calls on the name of the Lord will be saved" (Rom. 10:13).

Bible students will remember that *name* in Scripture is not simply a label or handle given to someone to distinguish him or her from another. Especially when used for God, name describes character or reputation. To call on the name of the Lord does not mean we need to say "Jehovah," or must know exactly when to call on the Father, the Son, or the Holy Spirit. To call on the "name of the Lord" is to look up or out or in to the one who is author of our existence. When a person looks to his or her Maker for mercy, the God and Father of our Lord Jesus Christ will graciously reply, without first requiring of the penitent soul a test in "Theology 101."

We are privileged to know the actual "name of Jesus." But is it not consistent with his Spirit that some who call on the Lord may only learn the literal "name of Jesus" on the other side of the grave? We have long acknowledged this to be the case with Old Testament saints. Does not God's justice call for an accountability based on the degree of light we perceived? All light (truth) is from God and is identified with Christ, who is called the light "that gives light" to every person (John 1:9). Can we not then believe that God may be doing saving work apart from us and our distinctly Christian formulations?

This does not take away God's "need" of us to do his work today, especially as spelled out in the "great commission." Love itself motivates us to share the best news we have ever heard. But we must honor the sovereignty of God by recognizing his ways as above ours. God is not captive to our form of his church. Heart repentance and a will surrendered to him are pleasing to God regardless of the external forms or language used.

Peter affirmed that there is salvation only in Christ (Acts 4:12). But this same Peter also said in the home of Cornelius,

> God has shown me that I should not call any man impure or unclean. . . . I now realize how true it is that God does not show favoritism but accepts men from every nation who fear him and do what is right (Acts 10:28, 34-35).

This is a bold statement, but fully in harmony with Jesus Christ himself.

Then Peter proceeded to preach, "Jesus Christ . . . is Lord of all" (Acts 10:36). These two emphases were not incompatible in Peter's thinking. We do well to keep them present in our thinking about peoples of other cultures and traditions. This is not an arbitrary endorsement of other religions. It is rather an insistence on the integrity and consistency of God. Repentance and faith are called for from all peoples equally, according to the level of their knowledge and understanding. We are all accountable for light received—not for light unknown.

It is also instructive to observe that Jesus did not single out any pagan religion for attack. His judgments were reserved for "the people of God" and their religious traditions. Yet there were numerous sects and cults in the region which could properly have earned his censure.

In conversation with the Samaritan woman, Jesus did not hesitate to assert the messianic lineage as being "from the Jews" (John 4:22). But he did not assail her religion in a polemic suggesting that salvation has to do with believing in correct doctrines. Rather, he offered her himself as "a spring of water welling up to eternal life" (John 4:14).

When Christians speak in the style of Jesus, they will not be occupied with judgments of others and their religions. We will not hesitate when necessary to point out significant differences or similarities to Christianity. But we will keep the focus on Jesus Christ as God's good news for all people. Criticizing others invariably stirs up a defensive stance against whatever we have to say. Then we come across as superiors, which creates a put-down of those listening to us. Sharing with others as equals inspires an openness to our message.

This equality is fact, not a psychological ploy to get others to listen. The fantastic diversity among people does not remove our essential equality as humans. We are equally dignified with the divine image, equally guilty of marring it by sin, and equally the objects of God's love.

It is foolish for Christians to sigh, "We have nothing in common with unbelievers." The above three great doctrinal principles fully establish our commonality with all people. We become "one beggar telling another beggar where to find bread." The arrogant paternalism is gone and people begin to hear each other—and their Lord.

The biblical teaching of hell and heaven is a loving message of warning and hope. It needs to be heard. Yet much mystery remains. Thus the message will not be well received if delivered with the smugness of one who presumes to know all the answers.

It is an ominous thing for finite creatures to reject the ways of the one who created them. There is an essential insanity about it. For even after the hellish consequences of hatred and warfare, lust and rape, covetousness and robbery have demonstrated what rejection of God's ways is like, we persist in our rejection! This persistent rebellion results in hell.

On the other hand, heeding the call of grace opens the doors of heaven. Sanity is restored as a person comes to himself (Luke 15:17) and returns to the Father's household (Luke 15:20). There the penitent sinner finds abundance with "music and dancing" (Luke 15:25)—a beautiful picture of heaven.

The evangelistic invitation is like the title of one of Karl Olson's books, *Come to the Party*! The ultimate banquet awaits you! Our call to the world is "Don't miss it! You are invited. A place with your God awaits you. Come and taste something of heaven today! Follow Jesus as your Lord. He is the way for both today and tomorrow."

So we must speak about ultimate destinies. Jesus, who alone fully understands about heaven and hell, has shown us that this belongs to the good news of the gospel. It will be included in our message if we are sharing Jesus' word, Jesus' way.

Reflection

A story is told about Albert Einstein's wife. She was asked if she understood her husband's theory of relativity.

"No," she confided, "but I know Albert, and I know he can be trusted!"

Her answer can be a clue for ours. Do I understand all about eternal life, about heaven or hell? "No," I must confess, "but I know Jesus Christ, and I know he can be trusted." If Christ truly arose, what does this say about his expertise in matters of life, death, and the next life?

Chapter Eight

Jesus Taught His Disciples

Jesus commissioned his disciples to "make disciples of all nations." He left them no manual of instructions about how to do it. Lacking courses in evangelism, they nonetheless proceeded to make disciples of all nations.

Michael Green once commented that the best "evangelists" in his church were often the folk who had been Christians the shortest time—and were not yet "spoiled by going to courses on evangelism or in reading appropriate manuals of instruction."[22] When the motive is strong, the methods are found. Filled with the Spirit of God's love, new converts eagerly share this love with others. Often they are quite effective. Until, that is, older Christians remind them how difficult it is to witness and how much training they need to do it!

Don't misunderstand. Training is important. New converts with more zeal than wisdom sometimes do more harm than good. But the zeal is not to blame. The picture as Michael Green described it would be affirmed in most churches. Motivation is the key. When there is gratitude to the Father for the grace of the Lord Jesus Christ, then in the power of the Holy Spirit disciples will make disciples.

Jesus the great teacher

There is, however, another important element of the disciples' effectiveness. They had a great teacher! Every student who has been influenced by an effective teacher knows what a privilege this is. It must have been a great delight for the disciples to watch and listen to Jesus teach. We can enjoy almost the same experience, as we study the teaching tools of the one whom most acknowledge to be the "Master Teacher."

What about Jesus' teaching held the attention and captured the loyalty of his disciples and countless others since? Stated negatively, Jesus was never boring. On the contrary, he must have been one of the most exciting and alive persons around. Whether his contemporaries agreed or disagreed with him, they always had to reckon with him. One disciple took his life out of remorse for betraying him; the others gave their lives out of loyalty to him!

Our Lord was at times enigmatic. Some of his parables were puzzling. A few pronouncements were shocking. But he was never dull! Most often his teaching was vivid and clear, challenging the heart, stirring the emotions, and illuminating the mind.

Ways Jesus taught

Let us examine characteristics of the way Jesus taught. Let us see what we can learn from him that will make our sharing of the good news both captivating and fruitful.

The first outstanding feature of the teaching of Jesus was the note of *authority* ringing through it all. People marveled at him, saying, "How did this man get such learning without having studied?" (studied formally, that is; John 7:15). "He taught as one who had authority, and not as their teachers of the law" (Matt. 7:29).

The answer Jesus gives us is, "My teaching is not my own. It comes from him who sent me" (John 7:16; 14:24). The first element of Jesus' authority was his conviction of a divine source of the knowledge he imparted. Confident in the truthfulness of what he taught, he inspired confidence in his disciples. One commentator has said,

> The authority which held the audience spellbound was not the magic of a great reputation, but the irresistible force of a Divine message, delivered under the sense of a Divine mission.

So lofty a claim would have sounded hollow had not Jesus' life so thoroughly supported his assertions. The real secret, then, of the authority of Jesus lies not in any technique he devised. The secret lies in his relationship with the Father. What he was made what he said convincing!

The authority of his words would mount in accord with the claims he made, provided they proved true. He did make staggering claims! Should any have proved false, so much the greater would have been the ridicule heaped upon him. His teaching would have lost its power. But because his claims were consistent

with his deeds, because his life so thoroughly supported his teaching, the impact was and remains impres-
sive.

Christians who follow the lead of Jesus will not
think of authority as something that sounds loud or
bombastic. Nor will they feel they must offer dogmatic
statements on all issues. Instead, they will confidently
affirm life with God. Their commitment to Christ has
convinced them that God's love spells hope for all
people.

Although far from perfect, they reveal a basic consistency between life and word which authenticates what
they say. It is this ring of reality that produces the authoritative note. Mother Teresa conveys more authority than most evangelists on TV today. Her life validates
her Christian confession. Integrity is the Christian's
mark of authority.

Spontaneity was a second feature of Jesus' teaching.
Everywhere Jesus taught—on the mountainside, by
the sea, in the synagogues, in the cities, in the temple,
along the way, to crowds, and to individuals. For Jesus,
teaching was a joyful and exciting adventure, whether
in a structured setting or in personal conversation.

It can be so for us. People in love cannot help talking
about the one they love. Michael Green puts it quite
simply when he says that the way to talk about Jesus
"is to be so full of the Lord that you can't help over-
flowing." Then he adds that "personal conversation is
the best way of evangelism. It is natural, it can be done
anywhere, it can be done by anyone. It is a shared experience when both learn and both teach."[23]

Jesus was always sharing what he knew to be the

mind and heart of his Father. He did not require a course in seminary before he felt qualified to speak about God. This should encourage everyone.

But while he spoke so spontaneously, it was always like an outflowing from the deep well of truth gained through personal acquaintance with his heavenly Father. So in one sense we could say Jesus was always preparing, through his exquisite sensitivity to truth everywhere. The "lilies of the fields" or "the birds of the air" became instant object lessons of God's providence as he observed these along the way. The world around him was his resource center.

Effective communicators delight in their art. Continuous learning is the best preparation for teaching. Good teaching in a classroom or in personal conversation springs from the overflow of truth's waters. Spontaneity is like the sparkle on these waves.

A third mark of Jesus' teaching was its *direct simplicity*. Recognizing the needs of people, he addressed them with disarming bluntness. Yet this directness was so coupled with a genuine concern that the "large crowd listened to him with delight" (Mark 12:37).

One reason Jesus' teaching was clear was that he used the principle of leading his pupils from the familiar to the new. For example, to those acquainted with the use of yeast in bread baking he said, "The kingdom of heaven is like yeast" (Matt. 13:33). To the fishermen he said, "The kingdom of heaven is like a net" (Matt. 13:47). Jesus started with familiar facts and experiences of life, then led his hearers on to the greater facts and experiences of eternal life.

Our challenge is to find and use those contemporary references that make good kingdom analogies. Robert L. Short has found many parables of the faith in "Peanuts," the Charles Schultz comic strip. A creative teacher will find numerous visual aids and other familiar items helpful in illustrating and clarifying the gospel. Billy Graham has the newspaper beside him as well as the Bible as he prepares messages.

"A good picture is worth a thousand words," but words too can paint pictures. If you have heard Kierkegaard's parable of the barnyard geese, you will remember it. Jesus offered similarly poignant parables.

Simplicity is not as easy to achieve as it sounds. Thought and imagination are required to put the great truths of the faith in easily understood forms. But love is eager to clarify these truths, so it takes up the challenge. Simplicity, clarity, and directness make for effective teaching. It was Jesus' style. Let's make it ours.

Brevity was a fourth feature of our Lord's teaching. Jesus was a master at pinpointing his teaching with amazing conciseness. In striking and epigrammatic fashion he drove home one of the most important truths of life.

> No one can serve two masters. Either he will hate the one and love the other, or he will be devoted to the one and despise the other. You cannot serve both God and Money (Matt. 6:24).

In many religions, the greatest teachers have believed that ethics are to be understood in terms of respect for the neighbor. But nowhere is this thought more positively or more *briefly* stated than in these words of Jesus: "Do to others what you would have them do to you, for this sums up the Law and the Prophets" (Matt. 7:12).

The golden rule further illustrates the nature of the brevity which Jesus employed. It was a way of focusing on the essential and avoiding the trivial. All the teachings of Jesus make a tiny book—but what a volume!

The art of brevity is important for Christian communicators, who usually must cope with stringent time limitations. In addition, the human attention span is limited. Beyond a certain duration, learning ceases. Said a homiletics professor to his students, "If you don't strike oil in the first twenty minutes, stop boring!"

A fifth and sometimes unnoticed ingredient of our Lord's teaching was *humor*. We read the biblical text with such solemnity that we often fail to see the sparkle that must have been in Jesus' eyes, or the smiles that must have formed on the faces of his hearers.

It took his four-year-old son to remind Elton Trueblood of this fact.[24] Matthew 7:1-5 was read during family devotions. The boy laughed. Not at something that distracted him, but at what he heard from the text. "Why do you look at the speck of sawdust in your brother's eye and pay no attention to the plank that is in your own eye?" The child was struck by the laughable image.

It is indeed preposterous to be so concerned about a speck in another's eye that we are unconscious of the fact that we have a plank (or log or beam) in our own eye. The child was right. Let's laugh at the absurdity of being one another's judges. Jesus makes the point unforgettable.

The same kind of humorous hyperbole appears in Jesus' comment to some of the religious leaders. "You blind guides! You strain out a gnat but swallow a camel" (Matt. 23:24). A teacher of less imagination might have said, "You leaders of others are incapable of seeing what is important, because you have no sense of proportion in terms of what really counts." But who would remember that?

The "gnat strainers" and "camel swallowers" are unforgettable. That was one purpose of Jesus' humor. Jesus did not joke with people simply to get a laugh. Instead, he often used a humorous edge to sharpen a point and make it memorable.

Harry Emerson Fosdick said, "Jesus did not jest as Socrates did, but he often let the ripple of a happy breeze play over the surface of his mighty deep." It is often easier to rid ourselves of our foolishness when we have been made to laugh at the absurdity of it. Gentle satire can accomplish this.

About thirty instances of Jesus' humor can be found in the Gospels. "A cheerful heart is good medicine" (Prov. 17:22) was a saying appreciated by Jesus. If our Lord could smile and cause others to smile—even while carrying out the most serious mission on earth—then he must have known something quite wonderful about the heart of God and the ultimate triumph of divine love and holiness.

So let us not ignore the role of humor in our teaching. Laughter and tears are not incompatible. Seriousness and reverence do not exclude mirth and humor. A good teacher will recognize and carefully use the gift of humor. We have a great precedent for doing so!

Jesus used a great variety of teaching tools but no reference to Jesus' teaching methods could omit underscoring his sixth and most popular one: the *parable*.

We have no record of Jesus preaching expository sermons, clarifying the Hebrew nuances of the text, delivering lectures on the authorship of the Pentateuch, or clarifying the "Relevance of the Red Heifer in the book of Numbers." I often wonder what Jesus thinks about the sermons preached each week. Is this really the method of teaching he would encourage?

In any event, when Jesus was asked, "Who is my neighbor?" he responded with one of the best stories ever told (Luke 10:25-37). The story even changed the definition of "Samaritan"—from undesirable character to good neighbor! When Jesus was challenged about his welcome to sinners, he replied with three great stories about a lost coin, lost sheep, and a lost son (Luke 15:1-32).

Rational discourse touches the brain, but stories from life touch us at deeper levels. Doctrinal lectures tell us about God, but stories introduce us to God acting among us in mercy and grace. Are the sermons we hear pedantic explanations of God? Or are they arresting glimpses of God acting out his salvation in the lives of his children?

Walter Wangerin has developed his gift as a story-teller, following in the steps of his master-teacher, Jesus. Wangerin's tale of "Ragman"[25] tells the story of Christ's death and resurrection more powerfully than any theological discourse I have heard. How could Jesus be pictured as a "ragman in the inner city?" Maybe the same way God is pictured as a searching shepherd, a careful gardener, a waiting father, or a merciful king by the one who knows him best. Almost a third of Jesus' teachings are in story (parable) form. There's a challenge to our teaching approach.

A seventh method Jesus used must yet be mentioned. He understood that the teaching process is not complete until the students can assimilate and reproduce what has been learned. Therefore Jesus made them participants in the action. They would learn best by *personal involvement.*

Jesus' followers could never forget the lesson on true greatness which Jesus taught them, not by a lecture or sermon, but by the dramatic action of washing their feet (John 13:1-17). Luke tells us that the disciples had been arguing about "which of them was considered to be greatest" (Luke 22:24). Then Jesus "poured water into a basin and began to wash his disciples' feet," taking the role of a slave. After this action he explained, "I am among you as one who serves" (Luke 22:27) and "I have set you an example that you should do as I have done for you" (John 13:15).

We are sent, as Jesus was, to be God's servants in this world. That means serving one another in the love and humility of God.

Jesus further involved his disciples in saying and doing what he had modeled for them by sending them into the towns and villages as his representatives. They were to announce the presence of the kingdom of God and demonstrate God's power with healings and exorcisms.

After this mission they returned to Jesus for an evaluation session. Jesus commended them. A good teacher knows the value of praise. He rejoiced with them in the defeats of Satan (Luke 10:18-20) but underscored their most important privilege as being the recipients of eternal life. The evaluation reviewed the results and established the priorities in ministry.

They reported on how the Word was received. This is the concern of a good teacher. It is not, "How did I do?" but "How did they do?" When they received the Word of God there was joy. The joy was not in the performance of the teacher, or the effectiveness of the healer—but in the "one sinner who repents" and comes home to God (Luke 15:7).

By this involvement with his disciples Jesus taught the meaning of the kingdom and how to share it. In this apprenticeship relationship the teaching process was accomplished.

The early disciples did well in sharing the message of the gospel with others in the Roman Empire. This was in large measure because Jesus had poured so much of himself into them. The presence of Christ was evident wherever they went (Acts 4:13). Since the training of disciples to disciple others was the central method of Jesus, it ought to be the major activity of every Christian church. Teaching and discipling go together (Matt. 28:20). Jesus' kind of teaching makes disciples.

Let's teach as Jesus taught, with authority, spontaneity, simplicity, brevity, humor, stories, and involvement. Disciples were made who reproduced themselves in others. "This is to my Father's glory, that you bear much fruit" (John 15:8) Sharing Jesus' word his way always bears much fruit.

Reflection

Personal involvement is the most effective method of sharing the faith. Thus perhaps we need to ask, "Am I meeting with another person, or a few other persons in discipleship training? If not, will I consider inviting a friend to join me in a series of studies in discipleship?"

This will mean more than studying and praying together. It will mean going out together to share the good news with a neighbor, or visiting a prisoner, or comforting someone in the hospital. Sharing the faith strengthens both the older and younger Christian. You might even ask the pastor to join you.

Chapter Nine

Jesus Prayed

Our Lord felt the need to pray. If he recognized that necessity, how much more do we need to cultivate the practice of prayer. What we ought to know about prayer, Jesus has taught. Let's consider his teachings.

In the New Testament, there are more exhortations to pray than to evangelize. Yet prayer is often relegated to a minor role in a church's life and witness. We affirm our belief in the efficacy of prayer but often do not practice what we preach.

Yet if we are genuinely interested in leading people into a living relationship with God through Jesus, we will need equipment that far surpasses clever arguments and successful methods. Regeneration is the work of God's Spirit. David Watson was on target when he said, "Prayer . . . is essential in . . . evangelistic work . . . to lift a person from the realm of argument into the realm of faith. Only the Spirit of God can touch someone with the power of God."

Prayer is the Christian's main way to appropriate the wisdom, direction, and power of God for sharing the faith. Prayer also prepares the hearts of those with whom we share to hear the good news.

No Christian denies the need for prayer. But prayer remains a puzzle for many of us. In our technological age, prayer seems naive and unscientific. Skepticism regarding its effectiveness deepens when we hear stories like this one from a young woman whose fiancé was a war pilot. "I went to church every day and prayed. I prayed every night and every day. But he was killed. I shall never pray again or enter a church!"

We appreciate her anguish and skepticism. Was she taught that her prayers would serve as protection for her fiancé? Why are some persons seemingly protected and others not—when prayers are offered for both? Was there something wrong with prayers that did not lead to the desired results? When we pray for the salvation of loved ones, does this guarantee their rebirth? The evidence does not always support this.

An amusing illustration comes from the little boy who prayed, "Dear God, If you made the rule that kids have to take out the garbage, please change it! Love Eric."[26]

We chuckle at Eric's prayer, but many of us secretly hope our prayers will cause God to change the rules for us. In praying for others, we sometimes hope God will override their will to accomplish our wishes for them. Will prayers do that?

Georgia Harkness once wrote, "Of all the things the world desperately needs, none is more needed than an upsurge of vital, God centered, intelligently grounded prayer." In view of the many pressing needs in this world, that is quite a claim.

Jesus and prayer

What is this "vital, God-centered intelligently grounded prayer"? We turn to Jesus as did his disciples when they asked that he teach them to pray (Luke 11:1).

The Scriptures record that Jesus prayed alone (Luke 5:16; 6:12; 9:18); with others (Luke 9:8; Mark 14:38); briefly (John 11:41-42); all night (Luke 6:12); in the wilderness, under olive trees, along the roadside, or in the temple. He prayed at regular worship times and before the duties of each day (Luke 5:15-16). He prayed before important decisions (appointing his twelve apostles; Luke 6:12). He prayed in times of crisis (Luke 22:39-44). His last words from the cross were a prayer. Prayer was as vital to Jesus as breathing is to our lungs. His entire lifestyle was prayerful.

It is startling to realize that Jesus, the Son of God, needed to pray. All his words and deeds, sermons and healings, decisions about life and death, grew out of power and confidence gained through communion with his heavenly Father. This tells us something about the place prayer must have, not only for sanctifying of our daily lives, but for accomplishing the church's mission in the world.

It is instructive to see what the apostles did after they received the "great commission." Jesus told them to "wait for the gift my Father promised," the baptism of "the Holy Spirit" (Acts 1:4). This would empower them for their task of witness from Jerusalem to the ends of the earth (Acts 1:8). We do not see them "sitting and waiting, but kneeling and praying."[27] This prayer meeting lasted ten days! They were prepared to wait on God for the fulfillment of his promise regardless of how long it might take.

The Spirit's descent at the baptism of Jesus was also preceded by prayer (Luke 3:21). The cable which channels God's wisdom and power into our lives and actions is prayer. With a task as colossal as world evangelism, it is vain and foolish to proceed without a great and continuous outpouring of fervent prayer.

If prayer is so crucial, why is its practice usually far from us? Tragically, we often do not recognize how desperate our situation really is. Another evidence of our faithlessness is spiritual laziness. We fail to appreciate that true prayer is work. We may also misunderstand what prayer is really about.

The priorities of seventeen churches in England, the U.S., and Australia enjoying unprecedented growth were surveyed. Prayer was the top priority. Unlike these churches, we often deny the supreme place of prayer in our actions even as we claim to believe in its efficacy.

In preparation for an evangelistic mission, for example, we think of our need of a good speaker, sharp advertising, adequate funding, an acceptable facility, large parking area, sufficient counselors, and, of course, a prayer-secretary, "because apart from prayer nothing will succeed." Then we go to work as if it all depended on us and our resources. What happens usually does.

Jesus did not depend on his own resources. Instead he cultivated prayer as a way to open himself to God's resources. And so prayer became totally natural for him, a constant, easily flowing conversation between him and a personal God. We see Jesus' interaction with a personal God in his favorite name for God—"Abba," which means something like "Daddy." Jesus' model shows that communication between God and his "children" is not only possible but natural.

Prayer begins as our response to God who has first addressed us. By praying we continue the conversation which God has initiated. In our prayer interactions we become increasingly better acquainted with God. Prayer is our heart responding to God's loving invitation to come to him. If this is the case, then silences and listening will become as important as words and speaking in the holy communion of prayer.

Basic elements of prayer

Let us simply recall a few basic elements of prayer. Prayer is a *godward orientation*, a conscious or unconscious "remain in me" (John 15:4). If prayer is only an exercise to which we turn now and then, it will be only that—a religious duty void of efficacy. But if prayer is the cultivation of an attitude of openness to God's presence in all of life, it becomes a dynamic force.

Prayer should happen *continually*, which is how Paul challenged the Thessalonians to pray (1 Thess. 5:17). This not only implied frequent spoken prayers, but a constant spiritual posture of openness to God's will. A wise Christian once wrote, "You cannot expect God to come into the occasional, if you refuse him in the continuous." The psalmist's call to "be still, and know" God (Ps. 46:10) is part of this relational attitude of prayer.

In church work, prayer *calms* the frenzied rush. It restores the discouraged witness. It brings to mind assurances from Scripture. It stimulates new hope. "Remain in me," Jesus said. "No branch can bear fruit by itself; it must remain in the vine. Neither can you bear fruit unless you remain in me" (John 15:4).

Prayer is the continuous *abiding* or remaining in God. It is not getting things from God so much as cultivating a right relationship of dependence on him. When we do not consciously depend on God, we inevitably rely on ourselves. Such self-reliance is a blight on the total ministry of the church.

Prayer is *surrender*. That was the one word the great Japanese Christian, Kagawa, used to define prayer. If we pause to reflect about who invites us into his presence through this special communication, we feel led to bow and say, "Thy will be done!" That was how Jesus prayed.

Often we think of prayer as a means of getting God to do our bidding, instead of a way to let us do his. Prayer is the surrender through which an avenue of new energy strengthens the disciple for obedient service. Christians come to believe that prayer not only releases spiritual influences in the lives of others but also has profound effects on their own lives.

When a sailor throws out the line to dock his boat, he doesn't pull the shore to him, he pulls his boat to the shore. Prayer brings us to the heart of God. Here we want to conform to his purposes. We do not suggest that God conform to ours. Here, close to God, we learn of his priorities and pray that they might become our own.

Often we do not fully understand how we ought to

pray. Then we are assured that the "Spirit helps us in our weakness. We do not know what we ought to pray for, but the Spirit himself intercedes for us with groans that words cannot express" (Rom. 8:26).

It is in this context that selfish desires are forgotten and our hearts open to the needs of others. For this reason Rosalind Rinker could write, "Prayer is the real key to love and communication; to learn to pray is to learn to love."[28]

The relationship to witness and evangelism is obvious. Here is where it begins! We bring loved ones and neighbors, friends or enemies, *first* to God in prayer. There God enables us to love them, shows us their needs, opens the appropriate doors for our witness, and enlightens and strengthens us for the task. The surrender of ourselves to God is our first step in giving ourselves to others.

Prayer is *affirmation*. In praying as Jesus taught us, we affirm that God is our Father; that hallowing God's name is our calling; that extending his kingdom is our duty; that doing his will is our daily assignment. Through prayer we learn that God cares about our basic necessities—physical ones like bread, and spiritual needs like pardon.

Through prayer, however, we are taught to pray not only for "my" daily bread or "my" forgiveness—but for "our" bread and "our" pardon. Prayer is *communal*. Through prayer we affirm our brothers and sisters and unite with them in a common concern for their physical and spiritual needs (social action and evangelism!).

We include the members of our faith community in our prayers for guidance, so that we may not fall into temptation in the time of trial. And we unite with all the church in a prayer for deliverance from all evil. "Give *us*, forgive *us*, lead *us*, and deliver *us*" is the way Jesus taught us to pray. Our evangelical and ecumenical responsibilities are underscored in each petition.

People sometimes ask what they can pray for. Does not Jesus' model prayer provide ample direction and content? Actually this prayer is more than a prayer. It is a creed for living. It establishes all of the highest priorities for the Christian and the church. Its order echoes the ten commandments.

1. "You shall have no other gods before me"	"Our Father in heaven"
2. "You shall not take the name of the Lord your God in vain"	"Hallowed be your name,"
3. "Remember the Sabbath day, to keep it holy"	"Your kingdom come" (the Sabbath for the people of God)
4. "Honor your father and your mother". . .	"Your will be done on earth"
"You shall not murder". . . .	

When we pray as Jesus taught us, we avoid grocery list praying which is totally self-centered: "Dear God, today I need this and that. Please deliver at your earliest convenience. Amen." Jesus reminds us to pause at the invocation and remember we are communing with our holy Parent. Our top priority is worship, to hallow the name or reputation of our God. We do this by joining in the building of God's kingdom, which in turn is achieved by doing his will in every area of life. When we do God's will, his lordship is acknowledged, his kingdom enlarged, and his name honored.

So Jesus shows us that the first concern of prayer is not our agenda, but God's. Yet, when we fall in line with his program and prerogatives, we discover our own deepest needs are met—and not ours only, but the needs of our brothers and sisters as well.

Those who pray are those best prepared for Christian witness. We know personally the one whose good news we bring. We can introduce people to someone we know. It goes even better when we realize that person is more willing to make himself known than we are to describe him. Prayer produces confidence for the task of witness. Prayer can even make witness a joyful privilege, for false pressures are removed. We are now prayerfully sensitive to the great Evangelist and those to whom he leads us. We are following God's direction and counsel as we share with those he has prepared for our testimony.

The prayer life Jesus modeled is a continuing relationship, a total surrender, and an affirmation of the Father's will. It is never an attempt to overcome God's reluctance but rather a recognition and appropriation of his willingness. God wills to answer prayer. He wills to impart his life to us. He wills to impart his life to others through us. Prayer is our participation with God in his gracious life-giving mission to our world.

Christ's ambassadors will find no substitute for the Word of God and prayer. Paul put it like this: "Take the helmet of salvation and the sword of the Spirit, which is the word of God. And pray in the Spirit on all occasions with all kinds of prayers and requests" (Eph. 6:17-18). To the Thessalonians he added, "Be joyful always; pray continually; give thanks in all circumstances, for this is God's will for you in Christ Jesus" (1 Thess. 5:16-18).

The effects of prayer

Joy and thanksgiving surround the life of prayer. These graces testify to the reality of the faith we share. The church which cultivates its ministry of prayer will have members prepared for outreach. When Jesus prayed, "the appearance of his face changed" (Luke 9:29) and "his face shone like the sun" (Matt. 17:2).

Prayer changes us, making us more and more like the one with whom we are communing. Such Christians bear a faithful witness to Jesus Christ. God uses us to bring others to himself.

After I had made a commitment of my life to Christ one Sunday afternoon in 1950, I felt led to tell Derrick and Joan Heatherington about it the same evening. They were the youth counselors of a church group I had participated in briefly.

They were delighted but not surprised to hear my testimony. "We started praying for you the first day you met with our youth group. We sensed God was at work in your life and now we rejoice in his answer to our prayers."

I cannot say how different things might have been for me had they not prayed. I can only affirm that I had a strong sense of their love and support. I believe God was working through their prayers to bring me to a conviction of my need and a conversion to my Savior.

Recently I attended a conference, sponsored by our denomination, for "developer pastors." We were provided with numerous guidelines, principles, and encouraging personal experiences of fellow pastors.

But Lon Allison, our director of evangelism, introduced us to an unusual participant. He was not an expert in church growth; he wasn't a seminary graduate; he was certainly not a professor. He wasn't even a pastor. He was a white-haired elderly Christian gentleman who believed in prayer and practiced his conviction.

He shared only briefly with us, but one thing he said came across with new impact. I had heard it before, but I have believed and practiced it more since I heard him say it. He said, "I'll give you two words to remember, two words that will make your churches healthy, that will cause your churches to grow. . . . These two words are *'protracted prayer.'*"

We can never share Jesus' word, Jesus' way without prayer.

Reflection

Augustine called the Lord's Prayer "the most beautiful part of the Bible." Luther added, "It is also the greatest martyr!" Vain repetition, thoughtless recitation, misapplied implications have pummeled this marvelous prayer. But when it is received as the word of our Lord, it lives to lift us to sublime heights in our ministry of prayer.

Since Jesus taught the model prayer, it reveals his priorities. With this in mind, think of the prayer not only as a set of themes for petition, but as a series of convictions for living. Its implications may become more clear when, as an exercise, we turn the prayer into a creedal statement. Try beginning each petition with "I believe in. . . ." The result will be not only a prayer to pray, but a prayer to live.

Chapter Ten

Jesus Worshiped

As we observed our Lord in prayer, we were seeing a worshiper. As we watched him value persons above traditions, we were seeing a worshiper. As we heard him reveal the "spirit" of the law beyond the "letter," we were seeing a worshiper. As we followed the Son doing everything according to his Father's will, we were seeing a worshiper.

It was not primarily his regular attendance in the synagogue, or his yearly pilgrimage to Jerusalem for the Passover Feast, that established Jesus as a worshiper. Certainly he would have worshiped on these occasions, and his participation in these celebrative events is an important example for us. However, worship had a much deeper meaning for Jesus than that which is limited to special meetings.

In fact, Jesus did not place special emphasis on attendance at religious assemblies. Nor did he command his church to meet for worship "at least twice on Sunday and once on Wednesday." Going to meetings does not a worshiper make.

Since the church is the "body of Christ" on earth, the pattern for our life and work is established by the model of our Lord. He lived to glorify the Father (John 17:1). When the church is compared to a building, it is called a "holy temple in the Lord" (Eph. 2:21) in which we offer to God the sacrifices of our praise. The church is first of all a family of worshipers.

The priority of worship

During the past several decades, the church has debated whether evangelism or social action is the most important assignment of the church. Worship was either assumed or relegated to back-burner significance.

Ronald J. Sider called for a balance between evangelism, social action, and other important ingredients of the church's life, including worship.

> The time has come for all biblical Christians to refuse to use the sentence: "The primary task of the church is. . . ." I do not care if you complete the sentence with evangelism or social action. Either way it is unbiblical and misleading. Evangelism, social action, fellowship, teaching, worship are all fundamental dimensions of the total task of the church.[29]

Sider concludes that evangelism and social action are of equal importance. Although distinct in function, they are equally necessary elements of the church's mission.

John R. W. Stott, who also assigns high priority to a Christian's loving concern for the physical and social needs of others, qualifies the partnership of evangelism and social action by a reminder that the Bible does teach the greater significance of the eternal welfare of persons over their earthly well being. "What good will it be for a man, if he gains the whole world, yet forfeits his soul?" (Matt. 16:26).

Thus the bread for the soul is ultimately more vital nourishment than bread for the body. But Stott would never allow this proposition to serve as a "cop-out" for Christians who withhold bread from starving people by spending their wealth on themselves. Offering both bread for the soul and bread for the body are actions of love. Both are therefore duties of the people of God. It is "the existential situation that will assign priority to one or the other of the two responsibilities."[30]

The parable of the "good Samaritan" illustrates the point. The victim of the robbers needed medical treatment, not a sermon. The Samaritan proved to be a "good neighbor" by meeting the need which was the most urgent at the time. Jesus calls us to "go and do likewise" (Luke 10:37).

I wonder if in the debate between evangelism and social action, we may at times overlook an even more imperative action of the church's life. Sider suggested a list of major elements in the total task of the church: "evangelism, social action, fellowship, teaching, worship."[31] Should we not place the last first? With full regard for the necessary interrelatedness of all these actions of the church, my conviction is that worship is primary. I believe this priority is rooted in both the Old and New Testaments and is clearly expressed in the teaching and example of Jesus Christ.

Many Christian writers, I suppose, assume the primacy of worship and proceed from there to discuss the church's role in the world—its "horizontal" dimensions of service. Others apparently forget or fail to appreciate how intimately genuine worship affects everything else we do. Out of over 100 messages brought at the International Congress on World Evangelization, only one included worship in its title. Only a handful made any significant reference to the place of worship in a church alive to its evangelistic responsibility!

I believe we ought no longer assume or ignore the supreme place of worship in our life together as the body of Christ. It is worship that inspires, informs, empowers, and directs our evangelism and social involvement. It is in worship that we are centered and strengthened for all tasks. Apart from worship we will get our priorities mixed and lose touch with the power of the Holy Spirit. Thus when David Watson discusses evangelism he says that "it is the foremost task of the church, *next to worship*"[32] (emphasis added).

More recently, especially in the charismatic movement, there has been an emphasis on the primacy of worship. It is thrilling to experience the marvelous expressions of worship at some of these gatherings. Whether by raised hands, clapping, or dancing, a new freedom is expressed by the worshiping community. The love and commitment of many participants indicates the reality of their worship.

However, genuine worship is not synonymous with its varied expressions. An emotional "high" is not necessarily true worship. Worship is much deeper. Its reality touches the heart of God in silence or in song.

Music will always be a vital part of a worshiping community. This was so in the first century (Col. 3:16) and is so today. Both hymns of the church and new songs have their place. But among some groups, music—and a certain contemporary style of music at that—is *the* expression of worship. Jesus' example tempers this emphasis. The one time we read of Jesus singing with his disciples is at the Last Supper. At the time he probably sang one or all of Psalms 113-118 (hardly "contemporary" songs!).

Worship was the central feature in the life and teaching of our Lord. When asked which was the greatest commandment of all, he replied, "Love the Lord your God with all your heart and with all your soul and with all your mind. This is the first and greatest commandment" (Matt. 22:37-38).

This call to worship is the foremost vocation of a believer. Our chief end is "to glorify God and enjoy him forever," as the Westminster Shorter Catechism has it. Jesus further stated it in his prayer, "This is eternal life: that they may know you, the only true God, and Jesus Christ, whom you have sent" (John 17:3).

The marks of Jesus' worship

What Jesus taught, he lived (Luke 2:46, 49). Jesus' overcame temptation through worship. Jesus challenges Satan with "It is written: 'Worship the Lord your God, and serve him only.' *Then* the devil left him" (Matt. 4:10-11; emphasis added). This is the *victory* of a worshiper.

Throughout his ministry, Jesus' frequent recourse to prayer emphasizes the priority he gave to his worship-

ful relationship with the heavenly Father. Jesus confessed, "By myself I can do nothing; I judge only as I
hear, and my judgment is just, for I seek not to please
myself but him who sent me" (John 5:30). This is the
humility of a worshiper.

Jesus was supremely interested in the glory of God.
"Father, the time has come. Glorify your Son, that your
Son may glorify you" (John 17:1). This is the *priority* of
a worshiper.

With the menacing shadow of the cross before him,
Jesus prayed in Gethsemane, "Father, if you are willing, take this cup from me; yet not my will, but yours
be done" (Luke 22:42). This is the *surrender* and obedience of a worshiper.

His last breath from the cross is breathed in worship,
"Father, into your hands I commit my spirit" (Luke
23:46). This is the *faith* of a worshiper.

The early Christians and worship

The first Christians were zealous worshipers. A. B.
McDonald has written of them,

> They possessed nothing more tangible than their congre-
> gation of worship. They had no buildings, no sacred book
> particular to them, neither a definite creed, nor rules, nor
> norms, such as those of Benedict or Bernard—they had
> nothing, except their worshiping congregations, which
> served as a stimulus for their loyalties.[33]

The book of Acts reports that

> every day, they continued to meet together in the temple
> courts. They broke bread in their homes and ate together
> with glad and sincere hearts, *praising God* and enjoying

the favor of all the people (Acts 2:46-47; emphasis added).

These worshipers turned the world upside down! Praising God in the temple or the marketplace, at home or on the streets, they found favor with others because of the reality of their relationship with God.

Notice the two ingredients that appear as a natural *overflow* of their worship. One is social action—selling possessions and goods, giving to anyone according to need (Acts 2:45). The other is evangelism—"the Lord added to their number daily those who were being saved" (Acts 2:47). Their fruitfulness was inevitable because they had the central issue straight. Love for God is completed in love for persons.

We all need a strong integrating core at the center of our lives, some supreme meaning to give meaning to everything else. We need someone to assure us of our significance and unveil some purpose for our lives. We need some overarching loyalty that can command our trust and inspire our hope. We are incurably religious and need some object or subject of worship. If the living God is not our Lord, we become lost in hopeless idolatry, choosing unworthy gods that only lead to disappointment and ultimate despair.

The people of the first century, like many today, had tasted the disillusionment of other loyalties and were struck by the joyful freedom of those first Christian worshipers. They had found their Lord—or rather, in Christ, God had found them! They now trusted the only one who merits total commitment from anyone. They celebrated this relationship in jubilant praise.

Those who were added to their ranks similarly became worshipers.

Worship that makes new worshipers

While serving a church in Prairie Village, Kansas, I received a letter written by an eighteen-year-old woman after she had participated in our service that Sunday. She related how God's Spirit had moved her to open her life to Christ as Lord and Savior. She shared something of her past life and her new found salvation. Then she added, "Thank you for letting me know that the Christian faith is joyful. I did not know that before!" The joyful praise of a worshiping congregation had made its own evangelistic appeal to this searching young woman.

Hector Espinoza has summed it up well:

> Worship should function as the means by which the people of God are built up in the Spirit in order to move out into the unredeemed world with an authentic, effective witness to the reality of God and to his great love made known to us in Jesus Christ. In the course of worship, even though it is primarily directed to the needs of the believers and represents the God-ward expression of the Lord's people, the unbeliever may well catch sight of God and thus be brought to faith.[34]

Evangelistic techniques that are mechanistic misrepresent the gospel. Those responding will be tempted to use the approach they first saw in us. So some may become "pushers" of their new faith. They may disrespectfully buttonhole others with their ten-minute formulas for salvation.

Others, embarrassed by such an approach, hang back in guilt. They believe they ought to share good news but are unable to use such unnatural methods. The analogy may be overdrawn—but as salespeople produce customers, politicians get voters, and entertainers produce audiences, so manipulative evangelists produce mechanical converts. *Only worshipers bring other worshipers into being.* If our evangelistic methodologies have suggested the salesperson, the politician, or the entertainer, then the results of our efforts will reflect these approaches.

It has been said that one-third of all Americans can testify to a new-birth experience. That percentage leaves me skeptical. But if there are that many Christians in America, what happened along the way to cause John White to observe that "North American Christianity is a religion without reverence"?[35] Like an ugly plague, irreverence and its accompanying disrespect for people or the environment has infected much of life.

Lamentably, this infection has also permeated the church. Even our theological seminarians are not immune. As a fine British scholar, John Whale, observed,

Instead of putting off our shoes because the place where on we stand is holy ground, we like to take nice photographs of the burning bush from suitable angles, or chat about the atonement with our feet on the desk instead of kneeling before the wounds of Christ.[36]

If we do not worship, neither will our converts.

Genuine worship admittedly remains at a low ebb. A. W. Tozer said that in many of our churches, "true spiritual worship" has been replaced by "that strange and foreign thing called the program." David Hubbard suggests three reasons why true worship is rare. As a people, he says, we are "infected by rebellion, idolatry and apathy."[37]

The rebel says, "I've had it." He is burned and embittered. The idolater says, "I've found it!" She has put her hope in some relative cause and limited goal which has become her substitute for the living God. The apathetic person says, "Who needs it?" and becomes indifferent and even insolent. Each reaction chokes off the response of genuine worship.

However, we must do something with our finitude and failure. We either attempt to cope in arrogant autonomy, making ourselves or some idol of our choice a god, or we bow in adoring surrender before the living God and become celebrants of life.

True worship includes all life

The late Archbishop of Canterbury, William Temple, once propounded a thesis that he admitted would sound fantastic and outrageous to many. He said, "This world can be saved from . . . chaos and collapse by one thing only, and that is worship." Maybe the dictum sounds exaggerated, even to Christians, but it takes on special significance when we hear Temple give his now classic definition for worship. He says,

> To worship is to quicken the conscience by the holiness of God, to feed the mind with the truth of God, to purge the imagination by the beauty of God, to open the heart to the love of God, to devote the will to the purpose of God.[38]

That is true worship. It is our total response to the "great commandment." Only in this context, with this love and loyalty, can the "great commission" be fulfilled according to the will of our Savior. Our "spiritual act of worship" is to offer our bodies as living sacrifices, "holy and pleasing to God" (Rom. 12:1). True worship is not limited to certain religious ceremonies, special music, or designated ritual acts. God is to be worshiped or served in *every* area of life.

The Bible establishes no watertight division between adoration of God and our daily work. Church bulletins ought not read at the bottom of the order of worship, "Worship ends, service begins." We must not separate what God has joined together. When we permit this division, our evangelism and good works lose their grace and power. Our prayers, hymns, and sermons lose their relevance. Evelyn Underhill put it well when she said, "Wholehearted adoration is the only real preparation for right action: action which develops within the Divine atmosphere, and is in harmony with the eternal purposes of God."

Jesus' epochal statement on worship was, incidentally, made during his "personal evangelism" of a Samaritan woman of ill-repute. Her ears were probably the first to hear that ". . . true worshipers will worship the Father in spirit and truth, for they are the kind of worshipers the Father seeks. God is spirit, and his worshipers must worship in spirit and in truth" (John 4:23-24).

To worship "in spirit" puts the emphasis on inner response rather than external regulation. Worship is not an engineered effect. Unless it proceeds from a humble and grateful heart, its external expressions will be sham and hypocrisy. Love, not law, draws the human heart to worship. Therefore place is irrelevant. Neither Gerazim nor Jerusalem, a cathedral or a cottage, can contain or limit true worship. The sanctuary in which the Father desires our worship is the temple of the human soul. The vital ingredient is spirit, not site. Thus Jesus frees worship from bondage to the letter, legal encumbrance, and ceremonial restriction.

To worship "in truth" emphasizes the need to hear the Word of God. Adherence to superstition, belief in falsehood, or worship of idols set no persons free. The Samaritan woman needed to learn that the one to whom she was speaking was the one able to give water that could satisfy her deepest thirst. To her query regarding the Messiah, she needed to hear Jesus say, "I who speak to you am he." This is how evangelism by a worshiper leads another to the liberation of true worship.

Our worship in spirit is our offering of ourselves to God through Jesus Christ, the true and living way to the Father. It is also offering ourselves to our brothers and sisters in the fellowship of the Holy Spirit.

Our worship in truth celebrates the marriage of wonder and work, of prayer and practice, of creed and deed.

To worship in spirit implies stimulation of zeal. The addition of "in truth" keeps zeal from becoming fanaticism and helps us navigate the straight and narrow road of a balanced biblical understanding.

Donald Gee put it succinctly, "All word and no Spirit, we dry up; all Spirit and no word we blow up; word and Spirit, we grow up."

In authentic worship, persons offer themselves to God and their neighbors in the sacrifice of love—through him who put together for all time the vertical and horizontal dimensions of love on the cross of Calvary. Only that worship has integrity which leads to concern for the deepest needs of people, as the highest form of "glorifying God and enjoying him forever."

To use worship as an escape from involvement with people in the arena of common life is to profane worship. To use evangelism without reverence as a way to get people to decide in our favor is to profane those we manipulate.

Rooting church growth in worship

The church does not need more programs of outreach or methods for winning the lost. There are numerous excellent sources for study. The church growth movement, pioneered by Donald McGavran, has provided invaluable research in this field.

Needed is immersion of all these church growth methods in an ocean of worship. We can then see which methods emerge as appropriate. People do not resent others sharing with them the most exciting and significant happenings in their lives. They do resent the implication that this experience must happen in the same manner to them.

People generally do not draw away from a gracious conversation about God. They do resent a conceited "holier than thou" attitude on the part of sharers. They generally do not resent an honest sharing of how Jesus helps them in and through failures. They do resent a profession of faith that does not square with failures they see in the ones professing.

We have many fine evangelistic methods presently in use in our churches. I encourage congregations to tailor their outreach methods by shaping them according to the spiritual gifts of their members. When they utilize the resources they have been given to meet the needs of their communities, they will see the fruit of their witness ripen.

Their leading question, however, should be not, "How shall we grow?" but "How shall we love?" That is the question which grows out of worship and keeps priorities straight. That question frees people from the burden of measuring results and releases them to wholehearted commitment of loving concern for all.

We need a new sense of the holy. We must indeed proclaim the gospel in the secular idiom, but we have too often secularized the gospel. We must remember that it is the gospel of God (Mark 1:14). The gospel is entirely God's. As stewards of his gospel, we are called to faithfully handle and share it. We are never authorized to do with the gospel what *we* choose.

Evangelism that is truly the propagation of good news finds its foundation in worship. In worship we are brought face to face with the character of God. We discover that he is the original Evangelist, the eternally first messenger of joyful tidings for all creation.

The flower children of the sixties were looking for love instead of materialism as the key to life. They were on the right track. Lacking a wholesome worship center, their bold experiment deteriorated into a malaise of drugs and disillusionment. God, however, loving these idealistic youth, helped many of them find Jesus (in most cases outside of the institutional church). One by one, many discovered in Christ the integrating center for the desired life of love and integrity. Then their numbers swelled to thousands and we called them the "Jesus people."

One of these "hippies," however, did make her commitment to Christ in an established church. It happened at a communion service in First Covenant Church in San Francisco. It went something like this. The pastor invited his congregation to think for a few moments about the health of their relationships. If any had offended or had been offended by another, they were encouraged to make it known so forgiveness and reconciliation could follow.

Hesitantly, one person rose to her feet and expressed her hurt over criticism some members had made of her husband, the choir leader. In response to her honest expression, several members went to her with sincere apologies. There was repentance and pardon. Then the reconciled family of God partook of the one loaf and cup.

That "flower child" in the congregation, who had thought church members were largely hypocrites, was so moved by what she had experienced that she ran (literally) to the front of the church just prior to the benediction. She said to the pastor, "Don't close this service until you help me to become a Christian. This is the love and reality I have been looking for!"

It was in the context of worship that God purified his own people and added to their number "those who were being saved." The pastor of First Covenant has told me that celebrations of communion in which someone doesn't become a follower of Christ are rare. Worship and evangelism go hand in hand.

While serving University Covenant Church in Davis, California, I received an unusual request. A young co-ed was having a birthday party in her dorm room. This was her first birthday since becoming a Christian. She wanted her friends to know how much her Lord loved her and all people. So she asked if I would serve communion at her party. She suggested the birthday pound cake could be the bread. And she had grape juice she would put in a glass for the wine.

I was surprised but couldn't resist such a request. Prayerfully I prepared myself for the most unorthodox communion service in my life. After a brief explanation of the meaning of the "Supper," I read the familiar words and served the group of about twelve students.

At the close there was total silence. I noticed some tears. I couldn't say anything for what seemed a very long minute. Then the girl who had wanted this sacrament for her birthday broke the silence. With deep feeling, she simply said,

"Y - E - A - H, GOD !"

Then we laughed and wept and hugged—for we had worshiped and were worshiping still. Those present who did not have a personal relationship with Christ learned it was possible and soon the "birthday woman" was helping others find new birth in Christ. A true evangelist is first of all a worshiper.

Worship releases our full potential

Let us deepen our commitment to a genuine worship of God. As we do, we know our place—his servants obliged to him for everything. As we worship, we also find our place as his sons and daughters, beloved and free to carry out his purposes in this world!

For this reason we must affirm that only in true worship can we find the full measure of our own potential. Only in worship can we find the release of God's redeeming power for ourselves and others. That is why true worship is always a joyful celebration, not only of the wonderful works of our God, but of God himself.

An old Jewish legend was retold by bishop Lance Webb. The legend suggests that Satan was asked after he fell from heaven what he missed most. His answer was, "I think what I miss most is the sound of trumpets every morning."[39]

The Bethlehem shepherds heard the angelic trumpets when Jesus was born. Paul tells us the trumpet of God will sound when Christ returns. The "poet-pastor" of the Revelation heard many trumpets in his vision of heaven. God's Word is celebrated in trumpet fanfare. That's his way!

So let us "sound the trumpet" more often as we worship our God and Savior. Others will hear it. Then by faith they will respond to the gospel and join us in the wonderful worship of God to whom belongs "the kingdom and the power and the glory forever. Amen."

Reflection

Collin Morris dreams of what worship could be.

The worship of men and women spending themselves in compassionate action would have an air more of desperation than formality. They would stagger into Church utterly drained of goodness, unable to face another day unless their numbed spirits were re-sensitized and their strength renewed. . . . Every false word in the service would stick out like a sore thumb . . . the most familiar truth would scorch. They would gulp the bread of Communion like starving men. . . . And they would not casually go through the motions of a ritual expectation of Resurrection on that first day of the week. There would be a heart stopping suspense as the service progressed. Would they really find a Risen Lord at work in the heart of the tragic mess to which they would have to return?"[40]

God calls us to rapturous celebration. We join not only the morning stars and angels in glory, but the very triune community of love—Father, Son, and Holy Spirit—in the song of eternal life! The melody is caught by others—first a few bars, then the chorus, then the stanzas until "a great multitude" exults:

> To him who sits on the throne
> and to the Lamb
> be praise and honor and glory and power
> for ever and ever!
> Amen
>
> Praise and glory
> and wisdom and thanks and honor
> and power and strength
> be to our God for ever and ever.
> Amen! (Rev. 5:13; 7:12)

Study Guide

This study guide has been prepared for small-group or classroom discussion of each chapter. The guide presupposes that the chapter has been read by each participant before attending the class.

In most cases, a few Scripture references have been added to enhance the Bible study part of the group experience. The questions have been designed for maximum participation. The intention is that these studies bring all members to the heart of each subject. The leader will be responsible to keep the discussions focused on learning to share Jesus' word, Jesus' way.

Jesus Identifies with Sinners

1. The writer of Hebrews tells us the Son of God desired identification with all people on this planet (Heb. 10:5-7). What is the stated motive? How does Philippians 2:5-8 support this?

2. John claims that it was when the Word became flesh that we began to see what grace and truth are really like.

How does the "flesh" or body enable us to see? (John 1:14).

If the church is the body of Christ, what should others see in the church? (Eph. 1:22-23).

3. The body is the tangible vehicle for the expression of the spirit, but the body itself is weak. How can the church affirm this weakness as a point of contact with the world—and still communicate grace and truth?

4. Immigrant churches from nations of different languages than English had difficulty identifying with their new neighbors in Canada or the United States. The "English" were considered "worldly"—and the idea of separation often meant having as little to do with them as possible. When the language barrier diminished, the challenge of identification became clear.

If ours was a church with this problem, how did we face it? If our church didn't have a language problem, how has it identified with its community in other areas?

5. Does opulence or extravagance look anything like Jesus? If not, how can our stewardship of wealth follow more closely the pattern of Jesus? In what way is a "rich preacher" a contradiction of the gospel? Should a different standard apply to the layperson?

6. Some people may be poor because they are irresponsible. Many more people are poor because they are underprivileged and exploited. How can we be a friend to the poor of each category according to the style of Jesus?

7. What actions can we take as individuals or as a church to affirm our solidarity with the people of our community?

Study Guide, Chapter 2

Jesus Balanced Word and Deed

1. As a study of all four Gospels reveals, the balance between word and deed in the ministry of Jesus is almost fifty/fifty. Since the church as the body of Christ introduces the world to the kingdom of God, reflect about its proportion of word and deed. Often it is

weighted on the side of words. What deeds or actions could we suggest to improve the balance?

2. The last parable Jesus gave, according to Matthew, is about the last judgment (Matt. 25:31-46). Study this passage.

    a. Notice our Lord's identification with all people at their point of need.

    b. Notice the role of word and deed in the actions condemned or praised.

    c. Notice the importance assigned to little things by our Lord.

    d. Is our church involved in these ministries?

3. No one congregation can meet all needs. Consider with gratitude what your denomination or association is doing at a broader level across the country and in the world. Learn of and pray for your denominational ministries of word and deed around the world.

4. List the most basic needs of people. Consider the special needs of children, youth, single, divorced, married, elderly, disabled, unemployed, retired. In what ways does our church address these needs? Where do our gifts lie? Effective ministries usually match the gifts or resources of a congregation with the needs of its constituency.

5. When it was heard that a church was to be built in my community, a petition was circulated to prevent such from occurring. A legal ruling favored the church, but this victory was not the best news. The true victory is that some opponents of the church are now glad it is here. They have seen how ministries of the church are helping young and old. Such a church is good news to its community. We all realize we are to

tell the good news, but the basic question must be, *"Are we good news?"*

What do the people of our community think about our presence among them?

Jesus Used His Bible

1. Read Paul's advice concerning Timothy's use of Scripture (2 Tim. 3:14-17). For what purposes was Scripture inspired?

2. What can we deduce from the way Jesus referred to the Old Testament? Discuss the values of his direct quotations and the significance of references he put in his own words.

3. What lessons might we learn from Jesus' selections of Scripture? Which parts should a Christian know best?

4. What are the values of Scripture memorization, especially in moments of crisis?

5. Sometimes we think of our use of various Bible translations as simply a matter of personal preference. If we follow our Lord's example in language use, we may find that using an up-to-date translation is more a

matter of obedience than of personal preference. Do you agree? Why or why not?

6. Does our church library have an up-to-date set of Bible dictionaries, commentaries, and other helps to Bible study? How could we help procure such for the church?

7. For Jesus, the truth of a passage was always bigger than the verbal arrangement. Sometimes we fail to see the forest for the trees. What sound principle of interpretation can we take from this example of our Lord (Luke 20:27-38)?

8. What does it mean for Jesus Christ to be Lord of the Bible? How do we let him guide us in our struggle to correctly interpret and apply the Scriptures?

Study Guide, Chapter 4

Jesus Makes Us His Advertising

1. You have heard Paul's statement, "by all possible means I might save some" (1 Cor. 9:22). "By all means" has been used to justify some strange methods. Often lacking is an understanding of the context of this verse. Read and discuss what Paul is really saying in this passage (1 Cor. 9:19-23).

2. Why and how did the following persons advertise the "good news"?

a. The once-blind man (John 9:25)

b. The Samaritan woman (John 4:39-42)

c. The former invalid from Bethesda (John 5:10-15)

d. Paul and Silas in Philippi (Acts 16:25-34)

3. Let us check our own newspaper, magazine, or TV advertising.

a. Is it truthful or boastful?

b. Is it glorifying our pastor (or another)—or Christ?

c. Is it in the language of the marketplace or in "Christianese," phrased in "King James" English?

d. Is it worth the financial investment?

4. How can we improve our advertising effectiveness? Some churches have encouraged members of their congregations to write a brief statement about what Christ and his church means to them. This is prepared, with a picture of the one sharing, and sent to the local paper as a paid advertisement for the church. This approach takes the risk of putting the fallible yet forgiven Christian on the line.

What do you think of this idea? What are some others?

5. How can we help one another to "talk up" the good news and verbalize the blessings we receive in Christ, so that it is neither forced nor artificial?

6. What does the phrase "body of Christ," when used for the church, suggest about its visibility and its advertising potential (Eph. 1:22-23)?

7. Are we accurate and helpful advertisements for Christ and his church?

Study Guide, Chapter 5

Jesus Gave an Invitation

1. To what does Jesus invite us (Mark 1:17-20)?

2. How does the concept of apprenticeship help us to understand the meaning of being a disciple (Mark 3:14-15)?

3. Discuss what ages we were when the role of Christ in our lives became serious. How did we understand his lordship at that age?

4. Share with each other how your conversion experience happened—suddenly or gradually?

(This was a question in one of my seminary classes. The results of the survey surprised me. Since my experience had been a "memorable moment encounter" with Christ one Sunday afternoon in 1950, I assumed everyone could recall such a moment. No. Almost half the class testified to a gradual and growing awareness of Christ's claim on their lives. Many could only say it happened during these months or that year. It was also obvious that Christ meant as much to those who came to him gradually as to those who came suddenly.)

5. How much information do you think prospective converts should be given before they are invited to receive Christ as Lord and Savior?

6. How do we understand "authority over demons"? How does our Lord help us and enable us to help oth-

ers to freedom from demonic bondage? What is the place of a personal decision in this matter?

7. Discuss the various ways of inviting people to make the Christian decision. Which ways have the most biblical integrity?

Study Guide, Chapter 6

Jesus Felt a Sense of Urgency

1. If you knew Jesus was coming tomorrow, what would you do differently today?

The story is told of John Wesley who, when a neighbor saw him hoeing his garden, asked a similar question. Wesley's response was that he would first finish weeding the garden.

Why do you suppose he made that reply?

2. What might help us understand the urgency of the hour—without driving us into a nervous frenzy?

3. What do we learn about timing from our Lord in the passage from Mark 5:21-43?

4. Share spiritually refreshing vacations. Why were they so uplifting? Maybe this will suggest guidelines for the next vacation.

5. What is the relationship between using our spiri-

tual gifts and meeting the needs of others? How does this modify the thought that we are responsible to "save" everyone?

6. How do we balance our days and months in terms of work and vacation, worship and witness, family times and times alone?

7. Since the needs of the world are great and the laborers few, how can we be responsible stewards yet appreciate the need for quiet time urged by Psalm 46:10?

Study Guide, Chapter 7

Jesus Understood About Heaven and Hell

1. I believe it was Nels Ferre who made the comment that he would not enjoy being in heaven if he thought his mother was in hell. As you reflect on that comment, consider this one by another theological professor. "To suggest that we all end up with the same reward is to liken God to a foolish university president who welcomes the incoming class with the assurance that it will not matter what they do while on

campus, they will all graduate with honors." What are these commentators saying about heaven and hell?

2. Discuss the way the spiritual law of the harvest works in daily life (Gal. 6:7-8). Is this a pointer to the life to come?

3. In what ways can references to hell be part of the gospel of love?

4. When some allied prisoners of war completed a tunnel to freedom, they were not met with challenges such as, "Is that the only way out? I believe there should be several ways. One way sounds too limiting."

The actual response was, "Thank God there is *a way!*"

That was also the response of the disciples, then and now. Moreover, if the one way is big enough to include all who long for freedom, what need is there for other ways? In light of this illustration, discuss the exclusiveness and inclusiveness of the gospel.

5. Look up the New Testament words for death. They will include sleep, departure, exchange, exodus, germinating seed, homecoming, victory, and others. Each is a wonderful hint about heaven. Consider what each says about that special meeting with our God and Savior when our pilgrimage here is done.

Study Guide, Chapter 8

Jesus Taught His Disciples

1. Having considered the authority of Jesus, share with your experiences of various Christian teachers. Who among them spoke with the most authority? What do you remember from them?

2. Since the best teachers are constantly studying and learning, what attitude does this require in the "student-teacher"? What do humility, openness, and flexibility have to do with this?

3. Those who have given children's stories in Sunday morning services know how much preparation goes into presenting a brief lesson. As an exercise in the art of brevity, have each member of the group tell the story of Jonah in as few words as possible. Or tell of the good Samaritan or the prodigal son. See who can say the most in the fewest words.

4. What are the values of humor in sharing the gospel? What do you think "holy laughter" means?

5. Study John 15:1-17 for clues to making our teaching effective or "fruitful." Remember, as we are all disciples, we are all teachers.

Study Guide, Chapter 9

Jesus Prayed

1. Share the various ways in which prayer can be continuous (1 Thess. 5:17).

2. How do we understand the idea of prayer as "surrender"? How does Jesus model this ingredient of prayer (Luke 22:42)?

3. Using the Lord's Prayer as a model or pattern prayer (Matt. 6:9-15), write out a prayer for your spouse, your church, your denomination, or anyone for whom you feel a burden. Follow each petition and insert the appropriate request according to the priorities of Jesus. This exercise will lift your prayers into more significant content than simply, "Lord, bless Bill or. . . ."

4. How does faith relate to prayer? How does each strengthen the other (James 1:2-8)?

5. Why is it often best to talk to God about a person before talking to that person about God?

6. Talk about prayer is often easier than praying. So why not take some time in this group session to pray. Follow the general order of praise, thanksgiving, confession, intercession, and petition. Encourage participation by suggesting brief sentence prayers. The "amens" by all are the faith affirmations that God hears and answers our prayers.

Study Guide, Chapter 10

Jesus Worshiped

1. Study the statement of Jesus on worship (John 4:23-24). In the context of conversation with the Samaritan woman, what do you think Jesus means by "in spirit" and "in truth" with reference to worship?

2. How does genuine worship affect our stewardship of the earth and all things?

3. How does genuine worship affect our fellowship and our evangelism?

4. What is the place and value of personal or private worship? How does the answer relate to corporate worship?

5. Is worship on the Lord's Day an exciting event at our church? How can it be more of a celebration in which we all participate?

6. How can contemplation of "the cross of Christ" deepen our experience of worship? Consider how Paul was led to worship by this focus in Philippians 2:6-11.

7. Study the songs of the book of Revelation (4:8; 5:9-14; 7:12; 11:16-18; 15:3-4; 19:1-8). What is the theme running through all of them? What does the theme tell us about today and tomorrow?

Notes

1. Rob Peterson, "A Gospel for Sinners," *The Covenant Companion*, Dec. 1990, p. 10.

2. David Watson, *I Believe in Evangelism* (Grand Rapids: Eerdmans, 1976), p. 95.

3. John R. W. Stott, *Christian Mission in the Modern World* (Downers Grove, Ill.: InterVarsity Press, 1976), p. 40.

4. Arthur P. Johnson, *The Battle for World Evangelism* (Wheaton, Ill.: Tyndale House, 1978), p. 18.

5. Edward John Carnell, *The Kingdom of Love and the Pride of Life* (Grand Rapids: Eerdmans, 1960), p. 149.

6. David Watson, *I Believe in Evangelism* (Grand Rapids: Eerdmans, 1976), p. 27.

7. *The Covenant Constitution.* From 1885 forward this has been the single unchanged confession of faith of the Evangelical Covenant Church.

8. Richard Stoll Armstrong, *Service Evangelism* (Philadelphia: Westminster Press, 1979), p. 77.

9. John White, *The Golden Cow* (Downers Grove, Ill.: InterVarsity Press, 1979), p. 77.

10. Douglas W. Johnson, "The Message and Its Medium," *Clergy Journal* (August 1970), p. 26.

11. Quentin J. Schultze, "Balance or Bias?" *Christianity Today*, March 18, 1988, p. 28.

12. Juan Carlos Ortiz, *Disciple* (Carol Stream, Ill.: Creation House, 1975), p. 12.

13. Robert Coughlan, *The World of Michelangelo*, Time Life Series (1966).

14. Arthur G. McPhee, *Friendship Evangelism* (Grand Rapids: Zondervan, 1978), p. 46.

15. Ann Kiemel, *I'm Out to Change My World* (Nashville: Impact Books, 1974), p. 23.

16. Helmut Thielicke, *The Waiting Father* (New York: Harper and Bros., 1959), p. 152.

17. Floyd McClung, "In the Pattern of Jesus," *The Other Side*, September 1978, p. 26.

18. McClung, p. 21.

19. Festo Kivengere—a paraphrase from a message I heard Kivengere share at the Covenant Midwinter Conference, Youngstown, Ohio, 1963.

20. Charles Swindall, *Killing Giants, Pulling Thorns* (Portland, Ore.: Multnomah Press, 1979), p. 79.

21. Alfred C. Krass, *Five Lanterns at Sundown* (Grand Rapids: Eerdmans, 1978), p. 152.

22. Michael Green, *Evangelism Now and Then* (Downers Grove, Ill.: InterVarsity Press, 1979), p. 117.

23. Green, p. 134.

24. Trueblood, *The Humor of Christ* (New York: Harper and Row, 1964), p. 9.

25. Walter Wangerin, Jr. *Ragman and Other Cries of Faith* (San Francisco: Harper and Row, 1984), pp. 3-6.

26. Compiled by Eric Marshal and Stuart Hample,

Children's Letters to God (New York: Pocket Books, 1975).

27. Bruno Hern, *Prayer in Evangelism* in *Let the Earth Hear His Voice* (Minneapolis: World Wide Publication, 1975), p. 1184.

28. Rosiland Rinker, *Communicating Love Through Prayer* (Grand Rapids: Zondervan, 1966), p. 85.

29. Ronald J. Sider, *Evangelism, Salvation, and Social Justice* (England: Grove Books Bramcote Notts, 1977).

30. Ibid., (John Stott's reply to Sider), p. 22.

31. Ibid., p. 18.

32. Watson, p. 11.

33. George E. Sweazey, *The Church as Evangelist* (San Francisco: Harper and Row, 1978).

34. Hector Espinoza, "The Biblical Mission of the Church in Worship, Witness and Service," *Let the Earth Hear His Voice* (Minneapolis: World Wide Publication, 1975).

35. White, p. 132.

36. J. S. Whale, *Christian Doctrine* (London: Collins Press, 1957), p. 146.

37. David Hubbard, article quoted from memory of a Fuller Theological Seminary Bulletin published in the late sixties.

38. Quoted in *The Covenant Book of Worship* (Chicago: Covenant Press, 1976), p. 13.

39. Lance Webb, *Disciples for Life in the Age of Aquarius* (Waco, Tex.: Word Books, 1972), p. 167.

40. Collin Morris, *Include Me Out!* (Nashville: Abingdon, 1968), pp. 36-37.

The Author

Randy Klassen was born in Winnipeg, Manitoba (Canada), in 1933. He was the eldest of three sons born to Mennonite parents who had immigrated from Russia a dozen years earlier.

World War II brought serious tensions to a German-speaking community surrounded by speakers of English. As a child, Randy experienced the confusion of belonging to a church which spoke the same language as the "enemy."

Through the witness of InterVarsity Christian Fellowship, Randy became a Christian. At age eighteen he was baptized in the North End Mennonite Brethren Church.

He received a B.A. from the University of Manitoba (1954), studied at Fuller Theological Seminary (Pasadena), and earned an M.Div. from North Park Theological Seminary (Chicago, 1959).

Between seminaries he was called to pastor Teien Covenant Church, Drayton, North Dakota, where he served almost two years. He was ordained in 1960. He served First Covenant (Winnipeg) for six years. Next he pastored University Covenant Church (Davis, Calif.) for five years. He was senior pastor of Hillcrest Covenant (Prairie Village, Kan.) for seven years.

Then he was elected to a four-year term as the denomination's executive secretary of evangelism. After serving his term, a marriage failure led him to surrender his ordination and leave the ministry.

He remarried and pursued a career in fine art. He and his wife, Joyce M. Klassen, have enjoyed success as Christian artists.

Randy learned much from seeing the church through a layperson's eyes. He enjoyed leading home Bible studies, counseling, and preaching without receiving remuneration or a professional label.

Then one Bible study began to grow. In 1987 Good Samaritan Community Covenant Church (Valley Springs, Calif.) was born. Suddenly Randy found himself back in full-time ministry. Humbled by personal failure and tested by the struggles of a lay Christian, Randy returned as a "wounded healer." The response was gratifying. Other hurting people found a church with whose members they could identify.

Now Randy was challenged to help form a church according to the biblical blueprint. Writing this manuscript became homework for his new assignment. His goal and the mission of Good Samaritan Church is to be a faithful expression of Christ's body sharing Jesus' word, Jesus' way.